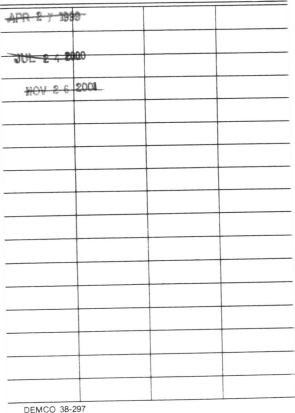

CRIMES OF THE AMERICAN NUCLEAR STATE

The Northeastern Series on Transnational Crime
edited by Nikos Passas

CRIMES OF
THE AMERICAN
NUCLEAR STATE
At Home and Abroad

David Kauzlarich
and Ronald C. Kramer

Northeastern University Press
Boston

Northeastern University Press

Library of Congress Cataloging-in-Publication Data
Kauzlarich, David.
Crimes of the American nuclear state: At home and abroad /
David Kauzlarich and Ronald C. Kramer.
p.   cm. — (Northeastern series on transnational crime)
Includes index.
ISBN 1-55553-371-X (hardcover : alk. paper)
1. Nuclear industry—Government policy—United
States.   2. Nuclear energy—Government policy—United
States.   3. Offenses against the environment—United
States.   4. Nuclear weapons—United States. 5. Nuclear
Weapons—Moral and ethical aspects.   I. Kramer, Ronald C.
II. Title.   III. Series.
HD9698.U5K38   1998
355.02′17′0973—dc21   98-23187

Designed by Joyce C. Weston

Composed in Veljovic by Coghill Composition Co., Richmond, Virginia. Printed and bound by Maple Press, York, Pennsylvania. The paper is Sebago Antique, an acid-free sheet.

MANUFACTURED IN THE UNITED STATES OF AMERICA
02   01   00   99   98   5   4   3   2   1

To Sandy for her years of love and support —DK

To my Mom and Dad, Doris and Bob Kramer,
with love and gratitude —RCK

CONTENTS

FOREWORD

Two generations of American adults, those who witnessed the rise of the Soviet Union to superpower status after World War II, and those whose earliest political consciousness was shaped by schoolhouse air raid drills, breathed a sigh of relief as the United States and the U.S.S.R. stepped back from the nuclear brink under Gorbachev's *peristroika*. They breathed another collective sigh a few years later as the Soviet Union vanished much like a paper tiger put to match. Congratulations all around! The United States had simultaneously defeated communism and eliminated the nuclear threat. As *Crimes of the American Nuclear State* makes abundantly clear, this is all too rosy a view of both history and the future.

The threats posed by nuclear states extend well beyond the dangers of nuclear war. Since the 1940s, however, the high drama associated with a largely manufactured threat of a preemptive strike by the Soviet Union served to eclipse the environmental and political damage committed by the U.S. nuclear state in the name of national security (Bottome, 1986; Lefever and Hunt, 1982). In recent years the environmental consequences of nuclear weapons production have become part of the public consciousness as clean-up problems surrounding sites such as Hanford, Washington, and the Savannah River Plant in South Carolina became increasingly well known (Carlisle and Zenzen, 1996; Makhijani, Hu, and Yih, 1995; Office of Technology Assessment, 1991). Likewise, increased public access to documents regarding radiation tests on uninformed or marginally informed subjects has further darkened the image of the U.S. nuclear state (Hacker, 1994). Less attention has been given, however, to the damage done by the nuclear posture of the United States to both democracy in America and liberation movements in less-developed world countries.

Blaming the nuclear character of the U.S. political state for the corruption of democracy in America and the suppression of liberation movements in the developing world may seem to be a bit of an analytic overreach. Indeed, I am not suggesting that other forces, particularly the processes of capital accumulation and the pursuit of American empire, were not important engines of this history. However, a critical reading of the past and a close reading of *Crimes of the American Nuclear State* underscore the extent to which official propaganda about the Soviet nuclear threat played a critical role in silencing critics of U.S. domestic policy and provided protective coloring for U.S. opposition to liberation movements that threatened the economic and political hegemony of capitalism in less-developed nations. Without the claims of a nuclear threat posed by the Soviet Union, it is unlikely that anticommunist sentiments would have grown to McCarthy-era levels. Yet it was just these anticommunist sentiments that halted the social democratic project that had begun during the Great Depression (Boyer and Morais, 1955; Caute, 1977), all but removed serious critiques of capitalism from academic and political discourse in the United States (Schrecker, 1986), and weakened public supports for movements for economic justice (Eckstein, 1997). Similarly, the use of U.S. power to destroy leftist movements in countries such as Greece, Guatemala, the Dominican Republic, Chile, and Nicaragua would have been less tolerable to substantial sectors of the American polity without the claim that these small, relatively powerless nations, if allowed to move left-ward, would become part of the Soviet Union's nuclear-backed plan to enslave the world under communism. Similarly, America's two failed attempts to destroy socialist governments—the U.S.-backed invasion of Cuba at the Bay of Pigs, and America's longest war (the war against Vietnam)—sought public support by claiming the need to curtail the spread of Soviet power, and in the final analysis, that meant Soviet nuclear power.

Truth may be the first casualty of a shooting war, but the history of the American nuclear state suggests that democracy was the first casualty of the Cold War. Instead of a nation governed by an informed polity, the United States in the post–World War II era became a nation governed by a military-industrial complex whose spin doctors manipulated public perceptions of the threat of a nuclear communism in accordance with the political and economic vision of an emerging American empire. This theft of democracy may be the ultimate state-corporate crime, a crime that shaped the character of the United States for the entire last half of the twentieth century, and created the context for a criminal nuclear state.

The legacy bequeathed to us from decades of an unbridled nuclear state is a grim one in terms of both the continuing consequences of past actions and the possibilities for nuclear wars in the future. Today we face landscapes poisoned by the effluent of a long history of nuclear weapons production. Here in the intermountain West where I live, battles over the transportation and storage of decades-old waste from nuclear weapons production and assembly facilities are contemporary and ongoing (Arizona Republic, 1998). This is not the only dark bequest of America's nuclear state. There are also people who suffer the effects of illegal or ethically questionable radiation tests, those who mourn the untimely deaths of loved ones who were victims of such tests, and the moral bankruptcy of fifty years of governance that has been willing to use nuclear blackmail—right down to the Gulf War—to impose U.S. will on the world. Nor are the problems posed by the nuclear state mere residues of the past. The U.S. government continues to use the threat of nuclear attack, now from terrorists or so-called "rogue" states rather than a superpower enemy, to sustain public support for the U.S. vision of a globalized capitalist economy and for a variety of domestic police-state countermeasures. In addition, nuclear weapons proliferation—begun by the United States—has increased the likelihood of nuclear war, not necessarily between the United States and Russia, but between other nuclear powers and their more immediate neighbors (Blackwill and Carnesale, 1993). It is these residual and future problems that make *Crimes of the American Nuclear State* a book that should be read by anyone concerned about the role of nuclear arms in the future of U.S. domestic and foreign policy.

Historians have sometimes argued that history happened the way it happened, and that to suggest things could have been otherwise is an exercise in the counter-factual. At the same time, it is the historical counter-factual that points to the possibility of finding alternative pathways for the future. By unpackaging the history of the crimes of the nuclear state, Kauzlarich and Kramer reveal the way in which these crimes need not have happened. They do this not by simply cataloging these past crimes but by providing a framework for understanding the context within which these crimes developed. By extension, they show what must be changed to preserve the future from a new round of nuclear crimes in the name of national security. Central to the authors' argument are two controversial propositions.

The first proposition is that we are not without legal standards to judge the crimes of governments even if no nation-state declares its own predatory actions illegal. Instead, Kauzlarich and Kramer argue that it is both possible and appropriate to utilize standards developed under customary international law and treaty to determine when a nuclear state is a nuclear criminal. In doing this, the authors transcend an ongoing debate among those who study corporate and political crime, to wit, how do we define legal yet wrongful acts without falling back on personal visions of right and wrong, morality and immorality? By relocating the debate outside the contexts of national law or personal morality, *Crimes of the American Nuclear State* offers a pathway around what has become a relatively unproductive argument among criminologists.

The second proposition is that crimes by political states are committed by *organizations,* not individuals. This latter proposition is as crucial to any strategy to reduce crimes by the nuclear state as it is controversial. It is typical of the American worldview, and of some criminologists, to assume that social outcomes can be explained only in terms of *individual* behavior. Indeed, Ronald Reagan went so far as to claim "there is no such thing as society, there are only individuals." This vision of human societies as mere aggregates of individuals leaves no options for addressing state crime other than to "throw the bums out." Since the middle of the nineteenth century, however, it has been a core proposition of sociological analysis that human social behavior occurs in the context of organizational arrangements that exert powerful influences on the behavioral options that appear possible and acceptable to individuals. Following this tradition, *Crimes of the American Nuclear State* demonstrates how U.S. nuclear blackmail, weapons-related environmental contamination, and illegal radiation experimentation cannot be explained simply by the malfeasance of those with their hands on the levers of political power. Rather, it shows how these crimes occurred within the context of organizational arrangements that made them both possible and likely. In the face of this argument, it becomes clear that any efforts to reduce the likelihood of crimes by the nuclear state in the future would require that we change the organizational context in which they grow, not merely the cast of characters in positions to commit them.

Crimes of the American Nuclear State delivers another message that I take to be particularly important: the crimes of the U.S. nuclear state are crimes of *empire*. In every case, they emerged as the United States sought to establish, expand, and protect its hegemony as the most powerful capitalist nation in the world. Empires have always been ruthless and dangerous when it came to maximizing their control over economic resources and human lives. Whether Roman, British, Chinese, Ottoman, Soviet, or American, imperial governments have often operated outside of the legal boundaries they establish for themselves, as well as the ethical boundaries of their age. The United States remains an imperial nation with nuclear weapons. There is little reason to imagine it is any less of a danger to the world today than it was during the period of U.S.–Soviet conflict. We may congratulate ourselves that we no longer allow our victorious soldiers to plunder the towns and rape the women they conquer. Yet our leaders feel free to discuss the incineration of hundreds of thousands of human beings in a nuclear flash as a matter of foreign policy and military preparedness, as if such a discussion were rational and moral. Such is the moral bankruptcy of empires.

By calling the *crimes* of the nuclear state by their proper name, this book takes an important step toward counteracting the growing complacency brought about by the recent deescalation of the Soviet nuclear threat. At the same time it does not join the calls for reinforcing U.S. global and domestic policing powers in order to protect the United States against terrorists and rogue states. Rather, *Crimes of the American Nuclear State* challenges us to refocus the nuclear debate on the organizational frameworks of the American empire that must be changed if we are to make any headway in ensuring that our nuclear past is not a prologue to our nuclear future.

Raymond J. Michalowski
Flagstaff, Arizona
January 11, 1998

REFERENCES

Arizona Republic. (1998). "Nuclear dump in New Mexico jeered." January 11, p. A28.

Blackwill, R. D., and Carnesale, A. (1993). *New nuclear nations: Consequences for U.S. policy.* New York: Council on Foreign Relations Press.

Bottome, E. M. (1986). *The balance of terror: Nuclear weapons and the illusion of security, 1945–1985.* Boston: Beacon Press.

Boyer, R. O., and Morais, H. M. (1955). *Labor's untold story.* New York: Cameron Associates.

Carlisle, R. P., and Zenzen, J. M. (1996). *Supplying the nuclear arsenal: American production reactors, 1942–1992.* Baltimore: Johns Hopkins University Press.

Caute, D. (1977). *The great fear: The anti-communist purge under Truman and Eisenhower.* New York: Simon and Schuster.

Eckstein, R. (1997). *Nuclear power and social power.* Philadelphia: Temple University Press.

Hacker, B. (1994). *Elements of controversy: The Atomic Energy Commission and radiation safety in nuclear weapons testing, 1947–1974.* Berkeley: University of California Press.

Lefever, E. W., and Hunt, E. S. (1982). *The apocalyptic premise: Nuclear arms debated.* Washington, D.C.: Ethics and Public Policy Center.

Makhijani, A., Hu, H., and Yih, K. (eds.). (1995). *Nuclear wastelands: A global guide to nuclear weapons production and its health and environmental effects.* Cambridge: MIT Press

Office of Technology Assessment. (1991). *Complex cleanup: The environmental legacy of nuclear weapons production.* Washington, D.C.: U.S. Government Printing Office.

Schrecker, E. (1986). *No ivory tower: McCarthyism and the universities.* New York: Oxford University Press.

ACKNOWLEDGMENTS

A number of friends and colleagues have provided support, assistance, and encouragement during the time we wrote this book. Our good friend Ray Michalowski (Northern Arizona University) provided constructive criticism, keen insights, and wise counsel. Thanks to Ray, this is a much better book than it would have been. David Friedrichs (University of Scranton) was an early and enthusiastic supporter of our work. His call, over ten years ago, for criminological research on nuclear weapons issues provided inspiration for our work. A special mention also goes to Bill Chambliss (George Washington University), one of the pioneers of research on state crime, for his inspiration and support.

Other good friends who provided support are Claire Renzetti (Saint Joseph's University), Dan Curran (Saint Joseph's University), Lew Walker (Western Michigan University), Rick Matthews (Ohio University), Brian Smith (Western Michigan University), Eric Johnson (Henry Ford Hospital), Nancy Wonders (Northern Arizona University), Diane Vaughan (Boston College), Stephen Pfohl (Boston College), Susan Carlson (Western Michigan University), Peter Yeager (Boston University), Hal Barnett (University of Rhode Island), Father John Grathwohl, Jeff Ross (U.S. Department of Justice), Steven Egger (University of Illinois at Springfield), and Stu Hills. Nikos Passas (Temple University), Series Editor, made many excellent suggestions that improved the book.

Special mention must also be made of Karen Rice (Western Michigan University), who did an outstanding job in preparing the final version of the manuscript. Her good humor and excellent administrative skills keep the Criminal Justice Program at WMU working smoothly. We want to publicly thank Karen for her great assistance.

Finally, Dave Kauzlarich wishes to express his love and gratitude to his wife, Sandy, and daughter, Elaina. Ron Kramer wishes to express his love and gratitude to his wife, Jane, and to his children, Andrew and Sarah.

1

Introduction: State Crime and the Nuclear State

> If we begin our work today by researching and analyzing state crimes . . . we will be on the cutting edge of a revitalized science. If we fail to do so, we will have little relevance to the world of the 21st century.
>
> — William J. Chambliss, Commentary. *Society for the Study of Social Problems (SSSP) Newsletter.*

> . . . [T]he almost total absence of attention to the nuclear arms issue by criminal justicians, in their professional capacity, may well represent both a lack of scholarly imagination as well as a gross form of professional irresponsibility.
>
> — David Friedrichs, *The Nuclear Arms Issue and the Field of Criminal Justice*

Is it possible for a nation-state or government to commit a crime? Can the use or threat of nuclear weapons be considered illegal? Can the production of nuclear warheads lead to criminal acts? Could state-sponsored human radiation experiments be a crime? Consider the following items:

- On August 6, 1945, a U.S. military plane dropped an atomic bomb on the Japanese city of Hiroshima. Many people were killed instantly; others died as fire swept the city. The official statistics: 78,150 people killed, 13,983 missing, 37,425 injured, 62,000 of Hiroshima's 90,000 buildings destroyed, and 6,000 other buildings damaged beyond repair. It should be noted that the City of Hiroshima's official estimate was 200,000 killed (Gerson, 1995, p. 26).

- Richard Nixon had a secret plan to end the Vietnam War: Threaten North Vietnam with nuclear weapons. According to his chief of staff, H. R. Haldeman, Nixon saw a parallel in the action Eisenhower had taken to end the stalemated Korean War. Eisenhower secretly got word to the Chinese that he would drop atomic bombs, and in a few weeks the war ended (Gerson, 1995, p. 115; Haldeman, 1978, p. 82).

- On July 8, 1996, the International Court of Justice, the judicial organ of the United Nations, ruled that the threat or use of nuclear weapons was illegal. This historic finding came in response to a request by the U.N. General Assembly for an advisory opinion. In the opinion the court stated that the threat or use of nuclear weapons would generally be contrary to the rules of international law (International Court of Justice, 1996).

- The nuclear weapons facilities at Oak Ridge, Tennessee, polluted the environment with about 800,000 pounds of mercury along with numerous other toxic and radioactive materials. Mercury-contaminated soil was used as fill at a local church and for a public school playground. Government officials and contractor employees who knew about the contamination were not allowed to alert the public (Gray, 1995, p. 8).

- Hundreds of U.S. citizens, including hospital patients and mentally handicapped children, were subjected to radiation experiments without their informed consent during the post–World War II era. These experiments were not as grotesque as those performed on prisoners by Germany during World War II, but the reasoning behind them was remarkably similar (Gray, 1995, p. 9).

The major thesis of this book is that many of the actions the United States government has taken with regard to nuclear weapons are illegal under international or domestic law and, therefore, a form of state crime. These state crimes concerning nuclear weapons can and should be explored in the field of criminology. Our goals in this book are to address the issue of illegal state acts related to nuclear weapons and radiation experiments, and to contribute to the emerging study of state crime.

Criminologists, government officials, and the general public have often been reluctant to face nuclear weapons issues. In their book *Hiroshima in America: Fifty Years of Denial*, Robert Jay Lifton and Greg Mitchell (1995) offer a powerful analysis of the unwillingness of Americans to face the truth about the atomic bombing of Hiroshima. They believe that "Americans need to confront Hiroshima and fill in the blanks of history" (1995, p. xiii). It is important not only to confront Hiroshima and Nagasaki, but also to examine the significant consequences that flow from the possession of atomic and nuclear weapons. Since the Japanese bombings, the United States has constructed a vast nuclear national security state that operates secretly, produces mass quantities of nuclear weapons, wields these weapons as an instrument of foreign policy to expand and maintain its "sphere of influence" (Gerson, 1995), and carries out nuclear tests and human radiation experiments on unknowing subjects. These developments need to be investigated, although for a variety of political and social reasons, most Americans prefer not to look too closely.

The denial and avoidance of nuclear issues extends to the

social sciences, particularly sociology and criminology. Kramer and Marullo (1985) have pointed out the paucity of sociological work on the nuclear threat, and two criminologists have noted the almost total absence of criminological research on nuclear weapons issues (Friedrichs, 1985; 1995; Harding, 1983). As Friedrichs (1995, p. 68) observes, "It is quite remarkable . . . that the vast criminal potential in the use of nuclear weapons has been almost wholly neglected by criminologists and criminal justice practitioners."

With this book we hope to end criminologists' neglect of nuclear weapons issues. Our purpose is to describe and explain a particular set of illegal acts engaged in by the United States government in relation to nuclear weapons since 1945. These illegal acts include the threat to use nuclear weapons in specific situations (what Gerson [1995] calls "nuclear extortion"), the process of producing these weapons which results in massive environmental contamination, and the conduct of human radiation experiments. These state-sponsored actions have caused enormous social harm and have violated a number of U.S. and international laws. We call this set of illegal acts on the part of the United States government "Crimes of the American Nuclear State."

Since our focus is on state crime, we start with a brief review of criminological perspectives on state crime. Among the most difficult issues to determine are: what is state crime, and is it really crime?

THE STATE AND STATE CRIME

Most sociologists define the state as a political apparatus that possesses a legitimate monopoly over the use of force and rules over a given territory. The term is similar to what most people mean when they speak of the government. In this book we will use the two terms interchangeably. Thus, when we speak of the state we mean the political apparatus of government; in particular, we will usually mean the offices, organizations, and agencies of the U.S. government.

The state, through the political apparatus of government and its agents, officials, and managers, historically has engaged in numerous violations of its own criminal and civil laws, as well as various forms of international law. Many of these state crimes have been exceedingly violent, destructive, and costly. Despite the frequency of state criminality and the enormous social harm it causes, the field of criminology has paid little attention to this form of criminal behavior; only a few criminologists have undertaken any empirical or theoretical work in this area. A recent analysis of criminal justice and criminology textbooks shows that "political" crime of any type gets very little coverage (Tunnell, 1993a).

Even when criminologists speak of political crime, they are far more likely to conceptualize it as a crime committed against the state (Roebuck and Weeber, 1978; Turk, 1982) than as a crime committed by the state. Likewise, some criminologists would classify state criminality as a subset of white-collar crime (Friedrichs, 1996) even though the vast majority of offenses that are examined under this rubric are occupational crimes or corporate offenses (Coleman, 1994), not crimes by state organizations or managers. The terms "governmental" and "elite" deviance have also been used in several textbooks to refer to a variety of transgressions by the state (Ermann and Lundman, 1996; Simon, 1995).

Much of the work on state crime has been done outside the boundaries of criminology. Sociologists such as Giddens (1987) and Tilly (1985) have done important work on nation-states and the use of organized violence, and Kelman and Hamilton (1989) have written on what they call "crimes of obedience," many of which are performed in response to orders from state authorities. Nonsociologists have also analyzed "how the government breaks the law" (Becker and Murray, 1971; Lieberman, 1972), from the crimes of the U.S. intelligence agencies

(Halperin et al., 1976) to state violations of international human rights around the world (Chomsky, 1987; 1988; 1993; Clark, 1992; Frankel, 1989; Herman, 1982; Stockwell, 1991).

The neglect of state crime by criminologists, however, appears to be changing. A number of works dealing with crimes of the state have appeared in recent years (Barak, 1991; Chambliss, 1989; Grabosky, 1989; Johns and Johnson, 1994; Kauzlarich and Kramer, 1995; Kauzlarich, Kramer, and Smith, 1992; Perdue, 1989; Tunnell, 1993b). Much of this recent work can be attributed to the influence of William Chambliss. In his presidential address to the American Society of Criminology in 1988, Chambliss introduced the concept of state-organized crime (acts defined by law as criminal and committed by state officials in the pursuit of their jobs as representatives of the state) and thus focused new attention on the topic (Chambliss, 1989, p. 184).

The majority of the criminological literature on crimes by the state has focused either on conceptual and definitional issues or on the nature, extent, and types of state crime. There has been minimal theoretical work done in this area. Ross (1995, p. 6) has produced an extensive literature review on state crime, and as he points out, "Unlike the voluminous literature on individual and organized crime, there is little material that aims at developing a model or theory of state crime, and much less that addresses and systematically analyzes methods for abolishing, combating, controlling, decreasing, minimizing, preventing and/or resisting state crime."

WHAT IS STATE CRIME?

As Friedrichs (1995) observes, a good deal of confusion surrounds the concept of state crime. Among the terms that have been used in this area are political crime, governmental crime, white-collar crime, state-organized crime, state-corporate crime, organizational crime, elite deviance, and crimes of the powerful. For clarity, we will use the distinctions set out by Friedrichs. His resolution to the conceptual confusion is to use the term *governmental crime* broadly to refer to the whole range of crimes committed within a governmental context. Next, he breaks governmental crime down into two specific types: "The term *state crime* will be applied to activities carried out by the state or on behalf of some state agency, whereas *political white-collar crime* will be applied to illegal activities carried out by officials and politicians for direct personal benefit" (1995, p. 54).

Friedrichs's definition draws a distinction between state organizations committing crimes to advance organizational goals, and individuals who use governmental positions to commit crime for personal gain. This tension between an individualistic focus and an organizational focus permeates the field of white-collar crime and the work of the field's founder, Edwin Sutherland (1949). In the area of white-collar crime, the distinction has been well accepted.

The organizational emphasis in the white-collar crime field became popular in the 1970s through the work of law professors such as Stone (1975) and Coffee (1977), and sociologists such as Clinard and Quinney (1973), Cohen (1977), Ermann and Lundman (1978a; 1978b), Gross (1978), and Schrager and Short (1978). Following the lead of organizational sociologists, they argued that rather than distinguishing the individuals who make up an organization, we should assume that the aggregated whole functions as a distinct entity (Hall, 1987). They asserted that organizations are real and it is reasonable to treat them as actors in the social arena.

From this perspective, organizations are real social actors for three primary reasons. First, organizations persist over time (Hall, 1987). An organization is a structure of positions that can survive the life span of a natural person (a term used for individuals as distinguished from their positions in organizations). Individuals occupy structural positions within a complex, formal organization, such as a government agency. But as Ermann and Lundman (1987) point out, it is replaceable people who occupy these organizational positions. Organizations can persist because the people who occupy positions within it are replaced on a regular basis.

Second, organizations develop norms and procedures (Hall, 1987). These norms and procedures direct or channel the behavior of the individuals within the organization. As Ermann and Lundman (1987, p. 5) put it, "the work-related thoughts and actions of people occupying positions within large organizations are powerfully constrained by the positions they occupy." The formal rules and informal culture of an organization shape the thoughts and acts of the people within.

The third argument for the reality of organizations is the presence of organizational goals (Hall, 1987). Most of the criminologists who study organizational crime emphasize that these crimes are committed to achieve organizational goals and not necessarily personal goals. While there is some controversy over the concept of organizational goals (Georgiou, 1973; Mohr, 1973; Perrow, 1961; Simon, 1964; Zey-Ferrell and Aiken, 1981), Hall argues that "the key aspect of goals is that they are critical components of the decision-making process, above and beyond the inputs of individuals and the external environment, and hence part of what makes the organization a reality" (1987, p. 86).

According to this perspective, not only are organizations real, but their existence has altered the structure of society and poses increasingly serious consequences for natural persons. James S. Coleman (1974; 1982) has described the emergence of corporate actors (organizations such as government agencies, business corporations, churches, and labor unions) and analyzed the way in which their existence has transformed the social structure of modern society. The chief result of these new structural arrangements according to Coleman (1982) is an "asymmetric society" in which corporate actors play an increasing role and natural persons a decreasing one. He goes on to point out (1982, p. 15) that "the emergence of this new structure for society has had and continues to have extensive consequences for the lives of the natural persons within it."

Coleman describes one type of serious consequence of an action by a corporate actor (such as a state agency) as risk. As he notes (1982, p. 79), "certain actions by corporate actors impose risks on persons increasing their chances of experiencing injury, sickness, or even death." Other sociologists have used the concepts of life chances and quality of life in discussing the actions of organizations in contemporary society. As Perrucci and Potter (1989, p. 5) observe:

> The way in which contemporary organizations carry out their activities has serious implications for the health and welfare of most Americans. Decisions made at corporate and organizational levels can affect a community's economy, health care, educational opportunities, environmental pollution, and social services, to name only a few things related to life chances and quality of life.

According to this view, then, organizations such as state agencies can be considered as real social actors who are capable of imposing risk on natural persons and engaging in socially injurious actions such as crimes. Therefore, despite Cressey's (1989) strong objections, most criminologists in the general field of white-collar crime argue that organizations as social actors can and should be the primary focus of analysis in research on state and corporate crime. This is the position we adopt in this book.

Finally, while most of our research deals with governmental or state agencies separately, often we will refer to the actions of these agencies collectively as the action of the "state" itself. The state as a whole is viewed as an organizational actor in its own right. In addition, we will on occasion need to include various corporations in our analysis. The concept of state-corporate crime has been advanced (Aulette and Micha-lowski, 1993; Kauzlarich and Kramer, 1993; Kramer, 1992; Kramer and Michalowski, 1990; Matthews and Kauzlarich, 1997) to draw attention to the fact that corporations and gov-ernment agencies can act together to produce serious crimi-nality. We define state-corporate crime as criminal acts that occur when one or more institutions of political governance pursue a goal in direct cooperation with one or more institu-tions of economic production and distribution. In chapters 5 and 6 we will describe how various private and governmental organizations pursue goals relating to nuclear weapons pro-duction and radiation experiments that intersect in such a way as to produce some form of social injury.

IS STATE CRIME REALLY CRIME?

We have taken the position that state organizations are real social actors that are capable of engaging in socially injurious actions. But can these injurious actions be called crime? Many government officials and scholars, including numerous crimi-nologists, would say no. We believe that the organized violence committed by the state has not been a central concern of crim-inologists and others for a variety of political, ideological, and intellectual reasons. But the most important factor in the ne-glect of state crime is the acceptance of state criminal law definitions of crime as the only legitimate criteria for the inclu-sion of behavior within the boundaries of criminological study. As Cohen (1990, p. 104) states, "Governments and their agen-cies do not commit crimes, but only because the criminal law does not take cognizance of them as criminal actors." He goes on to note that "they do, however, produce lots of noncriminal deviance."

We believe that this distinction between criminal and non-criminal deviance, however useful it is in the study of law and the social construction of crime, is not helpful in drawing the boundaries around the behavioral realities of crime. We argue that the classification of behavior as criminal for the purposes of scholarly research should not be limited only to state criminal law definitions, but can and should include other standards as well. Specifically, we contend that the principles and substantive content of international law can and should be employed as standards by which the violence of nation-states can be examined as a criminological question. This is why we regard the recent International Court of Justice ruling on the illegality of the threat and use of nuclear weapons to be so important (Kauzlarich, 1997; Kramer and Kauzlarich, 1997).

We start with the premise that no behavior is inherently criminal. There is no act that is in and of itself criminal. Criminality is not a quality that resides within behavior or persons. If one accepts this presupposition, then it follows that, in any arena we can identify (political or scholarly, for example), some definitional process is a necessary condition for the existence of "crime." Since criminal behavior is not preexistent, there must be some procedure that can be used to identify acts that are criminal and acts that are not. Every political jurisdiction, for example, must develop some legal mechanism to select out certain behaviors and define them as criminal (leaving other behaviors as noncriminal). Individual nation-states establish legislative bodies to pass criminal laws (effectively "creating" crime), police agencies to enforce these laws, prosecutorial units to bring charges based on these laws, and courts to convict and punish individuals who have violated these laws (thereby "creating" criminals). These laws and their supporting institutions are rooted in the moral values and concrete interests of those who create them or of their political supporters.

Just as state authorities follow a value- and interest-driven process to classify behavior as criminal for the purposes of formal social control, so too must criminologists follow a value- and interest-driven process to classify behavior as criminal for the purposes of scientific study. In the case of criminologists, however, there is no formal mechanism to create these definitions as there is within the state. Criminologists, therefore, are faced with a dilemma: how to identify behavior as criminal for the purpose of study? The easiest way, and the traditional way, is to simply borrow the set of legal standards created by the state. Thus, crime is conventionally defined as the violation of state criminal law.

By choosing this definition of crime, criminologists tacitly agree to use the moral values and legal norms encoded in state criminal law as the set of standards by which to classify behavior as criminal for the purpose of scientific study. This choice, however, implies a value judgment on the part of the criminologist that it is more appropriate for state authorities to select the behavior that criminologists will study than to allow criminologists to set up their own independent criteria. As Sellin (1938) pointed out, this clearly results in a loss of scientific autonomy for the criminologist. Furthermore, this choice to use a legal definition has important moral and political implications. As the critical criminologists have pointed out (Michalowski, 1985; Schwendingers, 1970), such a definition restricts criminologists to study those acts that are legally defined as criminal by the state, thus excluding other types of socially harmful and morally insensitive behavior, especially acts perpetrated by the state, ruling elites, and corporate organizations. As Tifft and Sullivan (1980, p. 6) note, "By assuming definitions of crime within the framework of law, by insisting on legal assumptions as sacred, criminologists comply in the concealment and distortion of the reality of social harms inflicted by persons with power."

On scientific, moral, and political grounds, some criminologists argue that we must not be limited to state criminal law definitions of crime in the study of criminal behavior. Criminology, they argue, must reformulate the definition of its subject matter so that all of the acts that violate emancipatory values are brought within the boundaries of the discipline. Such a definition will force criminologists to openly confront the moral and political choices involved in defining any act as criminal. The major problem facing this effort is the difficulty of translating the rather abstract emancipatory values used by the critical criminologists, such as freedom, social justice, equality, democracy, and solidarity, into a specific set of standards that can be used to classify behavior as criminal for theoretical and research purposes. How can we create a definition of crime that will bring organizational and institutional harms within the boundaries of criminology? Those who would advocate expanding the definition of crime beyond the categories of state criminal law must confront the vital task of delineating a moral and scientific basis for correctly applying the category of crime to socially injurious acts engaged in by the state (Schwendingers, 1977).

Over the years a number of attempts have been made to expand the definition of crime beyond the traditional criminal law approach (Kramer, 1982). Many of these attempts have been related to the issue of white-collar crime. For example, Sutherland (1940; 1949) argued that civil and regulatory law can be used to classify white-collar crime as "real crime." This expanded legal definition drew sharp criticism from some (Tappan, 1947), but it has become widely accepted by those who study white-collar and corporate crime today.

Some critical criminologists, however, insist that the definition of crime must be expanded beyond state definitions entirely. They have proposed a variety of "social" definitions of crime. The concepts of human rights and peoples' rights have figured prominently in these efforts (McCaughan, 1989). The Schwendingers (1970) were the first to propose a social definition of crime based on the notion of fundamental, historically determined, human rights. Others have followed the Schwendingers' lead in using the notion of human rights as the basis for the definition of crime (Galliher, 1989).

As the International Court of Justice decision on the illegality of nuclear weapons suggests, one fruitful avenue to consider in the search for an effective way to translate emancipatory values into a specific set of criminal behavior classification standards is in the area of international law. Many emancipatory values, peoples' rights, and human rights have received legal expression through customary international law and various international treaties and agreements (Akehurst, 1987; Ferencz, 1980; McCaughan, 1989). Michalowski and Kramer (1987) have suggested that to bring the transgressions of transnational corporations within the purview of criminological work, we should utilize the standards contained in the United Nations Draft Codes of Conduct on Transnational Corporations. As they note (1987, p. 47):

> The general principles outlined in the U.N. codes, as well as the specific provisions under each, provide a conceptual framework which allows us to expand the scope of inquiry without the epistemological hazards of definitions derived from personal conceptions of human rights. The U.N. codes represent the current stage of political struggle to refine the concept of human rights, and rights of national sovereignty, vis-à-vis large, transnational, corporate institutions. As such they are the appropriate reference point for understanding what constitutes transgressions by these institutions.

In the same way, we have previously proposed that the general principles and substantive content of various forms of international law constitute the specific standards that we use to classify the socially injurious actions of states and government agencies as crime for the purposes of criminological study (Kauzlarich, Kramer, and Smith, 1992). Support for this position has come recently from William Chambliss, one of the criminologists who pioneered the study of state criminality. As Chambliss (1995, p. 9) observes, "In this changing world, criminologists must develop a disciplinary vision which defines crime sociologically as behavior that violates international agreements and principles established in the courts and treaties of international bodies." In this book, therefore, we will develop a framework for the study of the crimes of the nuclear state based on a body of international law that, as the World Court has pointed out, can be related to nuclear weapons.

OBJECTIVES AND OVERVIEW

The purpose of this study is to describe and explain specific forms of state crime related to nuclear weapons. Our specific research objectives are:

1. To demonstrate that the general principles and substantive content of various forms of international law can serve as an epistemological framework for the study of state crimes related to nuclear weapons;

2. To describe the nature and extent of the following criminal acts by the United States government:
   a. the threat to use atomic and nuclear weapons during the Korean War and the Vietnam War;
   b. the massive environmental contamination resulting from the manufacture and production of atomic and nuclear weapons by the U.S. nuclear weapons production complex;
   c. the secret human radiation experiments carried out in a variety of locations and circumstances;

3. To place these governmental actions within a theoretical framework that allows us to identify and analyze the historical, structural, and organizational forces that shaped state decisions and explain why these crimes occurred;

4. To explore the issue of the social control of governmental

agencies and to ask whether such state crime can be prevented in the future.

Crimes of the American Nuclear State will deal with a variety of theoretical, empirical, definitional, and policy issues. We take a sociological approach in examining the problem of state crime in general, and nuclear weapons–related crimes in particular, within their wider social structural and organizational contexts. We also take a historical approach in considering the broader historical context of nuclear weapons policies and the tremendous role that these weapons of mass destruction have played in world affairs this century.

We begin in chapter 2 by sketching out the legal framework. We review the general principles and substantive content of international law and describe the historical development and contemporary significance of the body of international law relating to nuclear weapons. Relevant federal regulatory laws relating to the environment are also discussed.

The subsequent four chapters present the empirical case studies. Chapters 3 and 4 describe two threats by the United States to use atomic and nuclear weapons, comparing and contrasting the threats made during the Korean and Vietnam Wars. Chapter 5 describes the U.S. nuclear weapons production complex and analyzes the environmental contamination that has resulted from the routine operation of these facilities. The human radiation experiments that only recently have come to light are the subject of chapter 6.

The final chapter will pull these case studies together and offer a theoretical interpretation of the crimes of the American nuclear state. After reviewing the theoretical literature on organizational crime, we will offer an integrated model that we believe helps explain why such forms of state criminality are committed. In the concluding section of the chapter, we offer some suggestions for the prevention and control of state crime.

2

The Legal Framework

The International Court of Justice (ICJ) advisory opinion stating that the use or threat to use nuclear weapons would be illegal did not create new law. Rather, the ICJ decision clarified that existing international law, particularly the general principles and rules of international humanitarian law applicable in armed conflict, did apply to the use or threat to use nuclear weapons. This opinion, therefore, supports the argument that various bodies of international law can serve as a set of standards by which criminologists can classify behavior as criminal for the purpose of scientific study.

Criminologists who study more conventional forms of street crime rarely have to make explicit the legal framework they use to classify behavior as criminal for the purpose of study. This is due to the wide acceptance of state criminal law as a legitimate set of standards to use for this purpose. Those of us who champion the study of state crime, however, must provide a description and justification for the legal framework we use to bring state actions within the boundaries of criminology. The purpose of this chapter is to set out that legal framework.

THE DEBATE OVER THE ILLEGALITY OF
NUCLEAR WEAPONS*

The status of nuclear weapons under international law is a subject that has received a substantial amount of attention in the scholarly legal community. All of the scholars interested in this issue have approached the question by reference to the laws of war, which are considered legally binding principles to which governments are obliged to conform both in times of war and in their general military planning. The laws of war are essentially a conglomeration of principles based on the general postulate that humanity and proportionality are keys to protecting nonbelligerents in times of international conflict. They are also "generally aimed at protecting individuals and objects in armed conflicts against the effects and horrors of war" (Mohr, 1988, p. 83).

There are five basic principles of the laws of war.

1. in any armed conflict, the right of the parties to choose methods of warfare is not unlimited;

2. only as much force may be used as is required to overpower the enemy;

3. superfluous injury and unnecessary suffering must be avoided;

4. a certain amount of chivalry, fairness, and respect should prevail even in the relations between hostile parties; and

5. the use of weapons or tactics that cause indiscriminate harm as between combatants and noncombatants is prohibited (Bledsoe and Boczek, 1987; Lawyers Committee on Nuclear Policy, 1990).

*Much of the following section is based on an earlier article by Kauzlarich (1995); used with permission of *Humanity and Society*.

The laws of war are found in international agreements, treaties, and various customary laws. They remain intact despite the challenge that (1) the law is alleged to be vague or uncertain, (2) military necessity makes it impossible to comply with the law, (3) the opposing state is guilty of the same or other violations of the law, and (4) the law has been so widely violated that it is no longer binding (Miller, 1975). Thus, the laws of war are indeed based on legitimate legal principles interpreted by international courts as holding jurisdiction over the activities of a state (Bassiouni, 1992; Miller, 1975).

There are three main arguments that have been made by legal scholars, most of which were published between 1945 and 1960, to support the conclusion that the use and threatened use of nuclear weapons is legal under international law: first, that there is insufficient scientific evidence on the effects of nuclear weapons; second, that the laws of war have become impotent with the emergence of nuclear weapons; third, that there is no express prohibition of nuclear weapons (Meyrowitz, 1990). Each of these assertions will be reviewed and briefly critiqued.

The first proposition, that insufficient scientific evidence exists to reasonably calculate the effects of a nuclear bombing, is of course archaic. This argument is no longer employed to support the legality of the use and threat to use nuclear weapons. When Lauterpacht (1952), Stone (1954), and Tucker (1950) offered this argument to defend the legality of nuclear weapons, there indeed may have been limited information, especially to the general public, on the effects of nuclear weapons. The only available evidence on the effects of nuclear weapons at that time was the U.S. bombings of Hiroshima and Nagasaki, and this information was not readily obtainable during the 1950s. Given that the primitive atomic bombs dropped on Japan did not result in wholesale deaths of the entire country and that some individuals indeed survived these bombings, these scholars determined that the laws of war were not necessarily broken by the use of nuclear weapons.

This argument is no longer used to support the legality of nuclear weapons because we now have many studies establishing the general contours of the destruction that would be caused by the use of nuclear weapons (McNaught, 1984; Office of Technology Assessment, 1972; Perdue, 1989; United Nations, 1980, 1990; World Health Organization, 1987). Perdue, after reviewing the scientific evidence, concluded the following:

> In the event of a major exchange, estimates of quick death range from several hundred million people to the World Health Organization's figure of 1.1 billion people. The number of critically injured who would require available health care would perhaps approach another 1 billion persons. Given such an event, the basic services and organizations of society would collapse. Medical care, water, electricity, fuel transportation, communication, food supplies, sanitation, and civil services would all be devastated. (1989, p. 73)

The second argument in defense of the legal status of nuclear weapons is that the laws of war have become obsolete in the nuclear age. Claimed by such scholars as Stowell (1945), Thomas (1946), Borchard (1946), and Baxter (1953), this contention is based on the assumption that many of the laws of war were written prior to the genesis of the atomic weapon, and thus are not subject to the laws regulating contemporary governmental military planning. While it is undoubtedly true that some of the principles of the laws of war were penned prior to the nuclear age, these laws have been consistently interpreted by both scholars and the courts (including the 1996 ICJ opinion) as attempts to control any weapons or any method of warfare. In like manner, one need only note that while the U.S. Constitution's framers were not cognizant of all potential issues when creating the Bill of Rights, the basic principles of the Constitution are continually used to judge the lawfulness of actions (Meyrowitz, 1990).

It is argued by many legal scholars that since international laws not concerning the laws of war have been interpreted as binding on new technological and political developments, so too do the laws of war hold jurisdiction over nuclear weapons (Meyrowitz, 1990). Additionally, one must consider that a significant amount of the conventional laws of war have been developed in the age of nuclear weapons. Examples include the Genocide Convention and the Geneva Conventions.

The third argument in defense of the legality of nuclear weapons is that there exists no express prohibition of nuclear weapons in the body of international law. Thus, scholars such as O'Brien (1961) and Schwartzenberger (1958) argue that since there is no treaty, convention, or other international agreement specifically prohibiting the threat to use and actual use of nuclear weapons, one must conclude that these weapons and corresponding policies are lawful. This argument becomes flawed when one considers that the entire history of domestic, municipal, and international law is based on precedent setting in which new behaviors are constantly being weighed against existing principles of law. For example, one can imagine the foolishness of a defendant's claim that he or she did not commit a murder because he or she killed someone in a fashion not specifically prohibited by law. Under this logic, anyone who purposefully kills another by using, for example, computer disks to bludgeon or videocassette tape to strangle would be inculpable because the law does not specifically prohibit killing by computer disks or videocassette tape. International courts have consistently allowed the interpretation of behaviors not explicitly prohibited by law to be subject to existing law.

The three arguments used to justify the legality of nuclear weapons have little support in the academic legal community.

They have been reviewed and briefly critiqued here in order to demonstrate that the legal status of nuclear weapons under international law is neither a new nor an ignored issue in the legal community.

LEGAL STANDARDS RELATING TO THE USE OF NUCLEAR WEAPONS

Conventional Law

Some of the most important frameworks in judging the legality of a state's actions are the conventions that have been signed and ratified by subscribing governments. By accepting the provisions of a treaty or convention, a state is obligated to comply with both its spirit and specific prohibitions. Three legally binding frameworks have been noted by legal scholars with regard to nuclear weapons (Bilder, 1984; Boyle, 1987; Falk, 1983; Feinrider, 1982; Lawyers Committee on Nuclear Policy, 1990; Meyrowitz 1981, 1990; Miller and Feinrider, 1984; Mohr, 1988; Vickman, 1988; Weston 1983; 1983a):

1. The 1925 Geneva Protocol for the Prohibition of the Use in War of Asphyxiating, Poisonous, or Other Gases, and of Bacteriological Methods of Warfare (the Geneva Gas Protocol);

2. The 1948 United Nations Convention on the Prevention and Punishment of the Crime of Genocide (the Genocide Convention); and

3. The 1949 Geneva Conventions (I–IV).

Table 1 documents the year each of these agreements entered into force, the dates in which the United States became legally obligated to comply with these agreements, and the relevant substantive prohibitions found within these agreements. The Geneva Gas Protocol, Genocide Convention, and Geneva Conventions have been interpreted by many legal scholars as

Table 1
Treaties and Conventions Applicable in Determining the Legality of U.S. Nuclear Weapons Policy

1925 Geneva Gas Protocol

Entered into force: February 8, 1928

United States ratified: April 10, 1975

Relevant prohibitions: The use of asphyxiating, poisonous, or other gases, and all analogous liquid materials or devices

1948 Genocide Convention

Entered into force: January 12, 1951

United States ratified: October 14, 1988

Relevant prohibitions: Conspiracy, attempt, complicity, incitement, and actual execution of genocide.

1949 Geneva Conventions (I–IV)

Entered into force: October 21, 1950

United States ratified: August 12, 1955

Relevant prohibitions: Violence to life and person, mutilation, cruel treatment and torture of combatants and civilians.

constituting the specific prohibitions outlawing prima facie the existence of nuclear weapons (Lawyers Committee on Nuclear Policy, 1990; Meyrowitz 1981, 1990; Mohr, 1988; Vickman, 1988; Weston 1983). Because nuclear weapons are analogous to poisonous gas (the Geneva Gas Protocol), capable of exterminating an entire ethnic or racial group (the Genocide Convention), and would cause violent death and mutilation (the Geneva Conventions), it is clear that the actual use of these weapons of mass destruction would violate legally binding international laws. Again, this conclusion has been reached by the majority of scholars working in this area.

Customary International Law

Despite the importance of international agreements in the contemporary development of the law, any work concerning the laws of war which is limited to international agreements runs the risk of distorting not only the form but also the substance of the law. The codification of rules into particular agreements which began to occur in the second half of the nineteenth century did not displace customary law. (Roberts and Guelff, 1982, p. 4)

There are numerous sources of customary international law in determining the legality of the use of nuclear weapons. The classic statement of the role of customary law is found in the famous Martens Clause of the 1907 Hague Convention IV:

Until a more complete code of the laws of war has been issued, the High Contracting Parties deem it expedient to declare that, in cases not included in the Regulations adopted by them, the inhabitants and belligerents remain under the protection of the rule of the principles of law of nations, as they result from the usages established among civilized peoples, from the laws of humanity, and the dictates of the public conscience. (Quoted in Roberts and Guelff, 1982, p. 45)

And as stated by the Nuremberg Tribunal in their deliberations over the genocidal practices of the Nazis in World War II,

The law of war is to be found not only in treaties, but in the customs and practices of states which gradually obtained universal recognition, and from the general principles of justice applied by jurists and practiced by military courts. The law is not static but by continual adaptation follows the needs of a changing world. (Quoted in Roberts and Guelff, 1982, p. 41)

Given these guidelines set by jurists in prominent international tribunals, it is clear that for some state action to be labeled criminal under international law, no specifically codified law need be broken. Thus, state actions can be viewed as lawful or unlawful to the degree that they violate basic codes of behavior as established and practiced by international audiences. As Meyrowitz (1990, p. 39) aptly asserts,

> The legality of nuclear weapons cannot simply be judged by the existence or the lack of existence of a treaty rule specifically prohibiting or restricting their use. Traditionally, legal rules, both domestic and international, have been interpreted to encompass matters not specifically mentioned or even contemplated by the drafters of those legal declarations. As a result, the legal status of nuclear weapons must be judged in light of the varied sources of international law.

Similarly, a Japanese federal court in 1963 ruled that

> It can naturally be assumed that the use of a new weapon is legal as long as international law does not prohibit it. However, the prohibition in this context is to be understood to include not only the case where there is an express rule of direct prohibition, but also the case where the prohibition can be implied from the interpretation and application by analogy of existing rules of international law (customary and treaties). Further, the prohibition must be understood also to include new cases where, in light of the principles of international law which are the basis of these rules of international law, the use of new weapons is deemed contrary to these principles, for there is no reason why the interpretation of rules of international law should be limited to literal interpretation, any more than the interpretation of rules of municipal law. (*Shimoda v. The State of Japan,* quoted in Friedman, 1972, p. 1690)

What then are the principles of customary law that are relevant to the use of nuclear weapons? The first principle is that combatants and noncombatants are protected from unnecessary and aggravated suffering. First articulated in the 1907 Hague Conventions, this principle is perhaps the most accepted limitation on states involved in military hostilities (Bailey, 1972; Miller, 1975; Singh and McWhinney, 1989; Weston, 1983). The second principle of customary law, also grounded in the Hague Conventions, is that the means of injuring an enemy are not unlimited and that distinction must be made between combatants and civilians at all times. Indicating the profound global support for the relevance of these principles was the unanimously passed U.N. General Assembly Resolution 2444 (XXIII) (December 16, 1965) which "underscored the need to apply humanitarian principles to armed conflicts" (Meyrowitz, 1990, p. 17).

Additionally, many states have incorporated these principles into their military manuals, a clear indication that these principles have gained nearly universal acceptance. For example the 1956 Field Manual published by the U.S. government contained the following provisions:

2. Purposes of the Law of War: the conduct of armed hostilities on land is regulated by the law of land warfare which is both written and unwritten. It is inspired by the desire to diminish the evils of war by:
   a. Protecting both combatants and noncombatants from unnecessary suffering.
   b. Safeguarding certain fundamental rights of persons who fall into the hands of the enemy, particularly prisoners of war, the wounded, the sick, and civilians.

3. Basic Principles
   a. Prohibitory Effect: The law of war places limits on the exercise of a belligerent's power in the interests mentioned in paragraph 2 and requires that belligerents re-

frain from employing any kind or degree of violence which is not actually necessary for military purposes and that they conduct hostilities with regard for the principles and purposes of humanity and chivalry.

b. Force of Customary Law: The unwritten or customary law of war is binding on all nations. (Quoted in Singh and McWhinney, 1989, p. 55)

The U.S. Department of Defense official manual also addresses the importance of the laws of armed conflict:

All action of the Department of Defense with respect to the acquisition and procurement of weapons, and their intended use in armed conflict, shall be consistent with the obligations assumed by the United States Government under all applicable treaties, with customary international law, and in particular, with the laws of war. (Quoted in Falk, 1983, p. 526)

Customary law, then, prescribes the manner in which states may conduct war (Bassiouni, 1992). To further buttress the relevance of customary law to the nuclear weapons question, a number of historic international agreements and U.N. declarations categorically denounce the use and threat of nuclear weapons. The most important of these declarations was the U.N. General Assembly Resolution 1653 (XVI) adopted by a vote of 55 to 20 on November 24, 1961. This resolution demonstrates the legal and moral sentiment of the majority on nuclear weapons at that time:

The use of nuclear and thermo-nuclear weapons is contrary to the spirit, letter, and aims of the United Nations and, as such, is a direct violation of the Charter. . . . Any State using nuclear and thermo-nuclear weapons is to be considered as violating the Charter of the United Nations, as acting contrary to the laws of humanity and as committing a crime against mankind and civilization. The use of nuclear and thermo-nuclear weapons would exceed the scope of war and cause indiscriminate suffering and destruction to mankind and civilization. (Quoted in Meyrowitz, 1990, p. 26)

Other resolutions of the U.N. General Assembly demonstrate the international community's opposition to nuclear weapons (Meyrowitz, 1990; Riggs and Plano, 1988). Of particular importance is Resolution 808 (IX) passed on November 4, 1954 by a vote of 57 to 1 which called for "the total prohibition of the use and manufacture of nuclear weapons and weapons of mass destruction." While U.N. General Assembly resolutions normally do not have the force of law in a strict sense, they may have legal force "if they are regarded as statements of customary international law or authoritative interpretations of the U.N. Charter" (Riggs and Plano, 1988, p. 23).

Further buttressing the contention that the use of nuclear weapons transgresses customary international law is the case of *Shimoda v. The State of Japan* (1963), which is the only instance of a governmental court action (prior to the ICJ action) addressing the legality of the use of nuclear weapons. In a class-action suit, family members and some actual victims of the U.S. bombing of Hiroshima and Nagasaki filed a grievance in Japanese federal court seeking damages for injuries sustained from the bombardment. The judges based their analysis on the lawfulness of the bombings, not on nuclear weapons per se. Nevertheless, the court ruled that the U.S. bombing constituted a violation of international law based on both customary and legally binding treaties. The court ruled that

> it is proper to conclude that the aerial bombardment with an atomic bomb of both Hiroshima and Nagasaki was an illegal act of hostilities under international law as it existed at the time, as an indiscriminate bombardment of undefended cities (section 8). . . . The atomic bombing of both Hiroshima and Nagasaki is believed to be contrary to the

principle of international law prohibiting means of injuring the enemy which cause unnecessary suffering or are inhumane (section 11). (Quoted in Friedman, 1972, p. 1693)

In relevance to U.S. law, the court ruled:

With regard to the United States, it is known that treaties are the supreme law of the land in accordance with article 6, paragraph 2, of the Constitution of the United States, and that customary international law is also part of the law of the land. Such being the case, it would seem to be a fair assumption that an act contrary to international law constitutes an unlawful act in the municipal law of the United States (section 2). (Quoted in Friedman, 1972, p. 1694)

The *Shimoda* case and the 1996 International Court of Justice ruling (mentioned in chapter 1), both legitimate legal decisions, lend strong support to the contention that the use of nuclear weapons violates existing international law. But what about the threat to use nuclear weapons?

ILLEGALITY OF THE THREAT TO USE NUCLEAR WEAPONS

The question of whether threats to use nuclear weapons are legal practices is best treated as qualitatively distinct from the question of the legality of the actual use of nuclear weapons. Having established that the use of nuclear weapons would clearly violate extant international laws, we will now explore the criminal threats to use nuclear weapons by the United States in the Korean and Vietnam Wars.

Perhaps most germane in determining the legality of the threat to use nuclear weapons, other than the ICJ decision, are the principles found in the U.N. Charter. The primary purpose of the U.N. Charter was to render the use of force between states unlawful and to end the scourge of war (Henkin, 1991; Swing, 1991). According to Henkin (1991, p. 38), the Charter "remains the authoritative statement of the law on the use of force (and) acts as a principal norm of international law." The Charter "constitutes basic rules of international conduct that all member states are ostensibly committed to observe" (Riggs and Plano, 1988, p. 24). The United States has been a member of the United Nations since 1945, the year the organization was created.

Chapter 1, Article 1, of the U.N. Charter states that the purpose of the United Nations is

> To maintain international peace and security, and to that end: to take effective collective measures for the prevention and removal of threats to the peace . . . and to bring about by peaceful means, and in conformity with the principles of justice and international law, adjustment or settlement of international disputes or situations which might lead to a breach of the peace.

Moreover, Article 2 of Chapter 1 (4) states that "All members shall refrain from the threat or use of force against the territorial integrity or political independence of any state, or in any state in which the United Nations is taking preventive or enforcement action."

As a source of customary and treaty law, then, the U.N. Charter clearly prohibits both the threat to use force and intentional breaches of peace. The only exception to the prohibition of Article 2(4) on the threat to use force is found in Article 51 of the Charter: "Nothing in the present Charter shall impair the inherent right of individual or collective self-defense if an armed attack occurs against a Member of the United Nations, until the Security Council has taken measures necessary to maintain international peace and security."

Thus, a state under attack is allowed to defend itself. Importantly, however, the right to defend is limited; it is only absolute until the Security Council provides an international plan of action to halt hostilities. The Security Council ultimately retains the authority to enact the specific responses to an armed invasion.

In the history of the United Nations, the specific legal meaning of the Article 51 exception in relationship to Article 2(4) has been defined in only one case: *Nicaragua v. The United States* (1986). Here the International Court of Justice ruled that Article 51 applies only when a state has been subjected to an armed attack. Specifically, the court ruled that "States do not have a right of collective armed response to acts which do not constitute an armed attack. If no armed attack occurred, collective self defense is unlawful, even if carried on in strict compliance with the canons of necessity and proportionality" (paragraph 237).

The conclusion is unavoidable, then, that when a country threatens or actually uses nuclear force against another territory, a criminal act has occurred (Bassiouni, 1992; Boyle 1989; Nuremberg Campaign, 1990). Since the occasions in which the United States has threatened to use nuclear weapons have not occurred in response to an armed invasion of the U.S. homeland, the instances in which the United States has threatened to use atomic weapons must be deemed unlawful. While it may be true that some U.S. treaty obligations treat the invasion of a U.S. ally as an invasion of the U.S. homeland, nuclear weapons threats are still illegal because of their violation of the principles of proportionality and necessity.

Another framework by which to judge the lawfulness of the threat to use nuclear weapons is by reference to the 1945–46 Nuremberg Principles. These principles of international law originated from the Allied prosecution of Nazi war criminals, and are considered legally binding rules of conduct upon all states (Baudot, 1977). Table 2 provides a complete reproduction of the prohibitions created at the Nuremberg Trials. What is unusual about the prohibitions found in the Nuremberg

Table 2
Substantive Prohibitions Found in
the Nuremberg Charter

The following acts are crimes falling within the jurisdiction of the tribunal for which there shall be individual responsibility.

(a) **Crimes against Peace:** namely, planning, preparation, initiation, or waging of a war of aggression, or a war in violation of international treaties, agreements, or assurances, or participation in a common plan or conspiracy for the accomplishment of any of the foregoing;

(b) **War Crimes:** namely, violations of the laws or customs of war. Such violations shall include, but not be limited to, murder, ill-treatment, or deportation to slave labor or for any other purpose of civilian population of or in occupied territory, murder, or ill-treatment of prisoners of war or persons on seas, killing of hostages, plunder of public or private property, wanton destruction of cities, towns, or villages, or devastation not justified by military necessity.

(c) **Crimes against Humanity:** namely, murder, extermination, enslavement, deportation, and other inhumane acts committed against any civilian population, before or during war, or prosecutions on political, racial, or religious grounds in execution of or in connection with any crime within the jurisdiction of the tribunal, whether or not in violation of the domestic law of the country where perpetrated.

Source: Roberts and Guelff, 1982.

Charter is not only the outlawing of malign conduct of belligerents in war, but also the significant amount of attention paid to the crimes of conspiracy, planning, and threatening to commit the crimes of murder and other inhumane acts. In its deliberations, the tribunal convicted many individuals, as well as organizations such as the German gestapo, of conspiracy to violate the principles of humanity and peace (Friedman, 1972).

While the magnitude of destruction and murder committed by the Nazis dwarfs the harm for which nuclear weapons have been responsible up to the contemporary period, this does not mean that the basic prohibitions and principles of the Nuremberg Charter are inapplicable to nuclear weapons. The basic argument used by legal scholars employing the Nuremberg judgement to adjudicate the lawfulness of the threat to use nuclear weapons is that since the use of nuclear weapons is a violation of international law (because of its disproportionality and unpredictability), the planning and threat to use these weapons must also be criminal. The legal analogy drawn is this: Much like a Nazi commander's preparation and threat to exterminate Jews and other ethnic groups, the strategies of nuclear deterrence and mutually assured destruction constitute preparation, planning, and threats to use weapons which, if employed in time of war, would clearly violate extant international law. Since Nazi preparations to commit unquestionably illegal actions is conceptually similar to the plans and threats of the U.S. government to use nuclear weapons, there seems little question that threatening the use of nuclear weapons is criminal under the legally binding principles of the Nuremberg Charter. As Falk (1983, p. 528) states, "To the extent existing doctrines and plans rest on a conception of deterrence based on threats to civilian non-combatants and non-military objectives, these (threats) would be illegal under even the narrowest definition of the applicability of international law."

LAWS PROHIBITING THE CONTAMINATION OF THE ENVIRONMENT

Historically the U.S. nuclear weapons production complex was not required to comply with any laws regarding the protection of the environment. The Atomic Energy Acts of 1946 and 1954 made this condition explicit. Today, the DOE, which now has all but halted the production of new nuclear weapons, is still exempt from many laws regulating the disposal and treatment of radioactive waste.

Since its creation, the Department of Energy (DOE) has regulated itself for radioactive releases into ground and surface water, radioactive waste, and radioactive leaks into water. In the 1970s, however, came three principal environmental laws with which the DOE was required to comply: (1) the Clean Water Act of 1972, (2) the Clean Air Act of 1970, and (3) the Resource Conservation and Recovery Act (RCRA) of 1976.

RCRA gives the Environmental Protection Agency (EPA) the authority to regulate DOE's hazardous waste disposal practices. Under RCRA, "an operator must identify its hazardous wastes; receive a permit in order to treat, store, or dispose of such wastes; monitor ground water at waste sites; close and care for sites that are taken out of operation; and undertake corrective action" (Reicher, 1986, p. 205).

The Clean Water Act is "the principal law governing the discharge of liquid fluids from DOE facilities into water" (U.S. General Accounting Office, 1986, p. 30). RCRA and the Clean Water Act are not mutually exclusive laws because most of the contamination of water results from the violation of RCRA, that is, illegal waste-disposal practices. In a 1986 U.S. General Accounting Office report that identified RCRA violations, noncompliance with the Clean Water Act was also cited. Of the nine facilities surveyed, all were in violation of the Clean Water Act. The water was most often contaminated with tritium, mercury, and nitrates. As with the DOE's violations of RCRA, the activities of the nuclear weapons production complex were being conducted in violation of the Clean Water Act.

There is very little information on possible DOE violations of the Clean Air Act. Although the DOE must comply with this law, the contractors, under the agreement with the DOE, are responsible for reporting possible violations of the Act to the

DOE. The DOE is then obligated to report the violations to the EPA. One commentator has suggested that the DOE is really given powers of self-regulation in this area (Alverez, 1990).

LAWS PROHIBITING RECKLESS HUMAN RADIATION EXPERIMENTS

The U.S. government has carried out thousands of human radiation experiments; U.S. agencies known to have participated or conducted questionable human experiments are the Central Intelligence Agency, the Department of Defense (DOD) (including the Office of the Secretary of Defense, the Air Force, Army, Navy, and the Nuclear Defense Agency), the DOE, the Department of Health and Human Services, the Department of Veteran Affairs, and NASA (Advisory Committee on Human Radiation Experiments, 1995). Most of the experiments were designed to discern the effects of radiation on the human body, and most of them were illegal under international law.

The major law prohibiting reckless and nonconsensual human radiation experiments is the Nuremberg Code. The Nuremberg Code was established by the International Military Tribunal at Nuremberg in response to Nazi atrocities during World War II. The codified portions of this year-long proceeding relevant to our analysis are the prohibitions against involuntary and nonconsensual human experimentation. The first part of the Nuremberg Code merits special attention, so we quote it at length:

> The voluntary consent of the human subject is absolutely essential. This means that the person involved should have legal capacity to give consent; should be so situated as to be able to exercise free power of choice without the intervention of any element of force, fraud, deceit duress, overreaching, or other ulterior form of constraint or coercion; and should have sufficient knowledge and compre-

hension of the elements of the subject matter involved as to enable him [*sic*] to make an understanding and enlightened decision. (Advisory Committee on Human Radiation Experiments, 1995, p. 103)

The Code effectively outlaws states and state-supported scholars and researchers from engaging in human experimentation without the full disclosure of all risks and purposes of the research. It also mandates that participants in studies are made reasonably aware of the methodology, duration, and ultimate purpose of an experiment. U.S. government agencies such as the DOD and the DOE have in the last two decades conducted their experiments in accordance with these principles. But there was little compliance with the Code from the beginning of the atomic age until the 1970s. While there were Atomic Energy Commission (AEC) and DOD regulations ostensibly protecting potential human subjects in the 1940s and 1950s, these guidelines were hollow. There was no enforcement or serious dissemination of the ethical and legal responsibilities associated with radiation research. In fact, some researchers reported that while they had heard of the regulations, they had never seen a copy of them in writing. Many other scientists were completely ignorant of the guidelines. Even in the 1970s, after the AEC mandated that human subjects give informed consent, there was no requirement that this consent be in writing (Advisory Committee on Human Radiation Experiments, 1995, p. 103).

The Nuremberg Code also offers several other protections to human subjects and further specific guidelines for researchers to follow. They include:

a) The experiment should be such to yield fruitful results for the good of society;

b) The experiment . . . should be based on the results of animal experimentation and a knowledge of the natural history of the disease or other problem under study that the anticipated results will justify the performance of the experiments;

c) The degree of risk to be taken should never exceed that determined by the humanitarian importance of the problem to be solved by the experiment; and

d) The experiment should be so conducted as to avoid all unnecessary physical and mental suffering and injury. (Advisory Committee on Human Radiation Experiments, 1995, p. 110)

We have found from a review of primary and secondary documents that many of these rules have either been ignored or transgressed in many U.S. human radiation experiments.

CONCLUSION

The various international and federal regulatory laws we have just reviewed constitute the legal framework to be used in this study of crimes of the American nuclear state. Our position is that all criminologists must select a set of standards to classify behavior as criminal for the purpose of study. In the study of state crime, this requirement is even more important, given that most people, including criminologists, are not familiar with the laws that govern state actions.

Given the laws we have identified, we are now ready to begin to examine a number of cases of government behavior that violated these laws. Whether these behaviors are "officially" defined as criminal or subjected to formal social control is more of a political question than a scientific one.

3

The Threat to Use Atomic Weapons during the Korean War

It is fair to say that the United States has not used atomic or nuclear weapons* since the bombings of Hiroshima and Nagasaki. In another sense, however, the U.S. government has indeed "used" nuclear weapons since 1945 by threatening to detonate them on numerous occasions. The strategy of nuclear deterrence is, in fact, based on the threat of a massive nuclear retaliation to an enemy attack. The United States also threatened the "first use" of nuclear weapons to defend Western Europe from a Soviet land invasion. The United States has also threatened to use nuclear weapons in an effort to resolve certain international confrontations, what Gerson (1995) calls "nuclear extortion" or "atomic diplomacy."

In this chapter and the next, we describe and analyze two specific situations where the U.S. government threatened to

---

*Atomic weapons are distinguished from the much more powerful nuclear weapons in that they operate under the fission principle, while nuclear weapons operate under fusion physics. The U.S. stockpile during the Korean War consisted only of fission weapons and thus this chapter uses the term "atomic" rather than "nuclear" weapons. Production of atomic weapons halted in 1954, when the United States launched production of the fusion hydrogen bomb.

---

use atomic or nuclear weapons in an effort to resolve an international conflict in which it was involved. Given the ICJ decision of 1996, which clarified that the use or threat to use nuclear weapons is illegal under international laws that predate the invention of atomic weapons, we argue that these two specific nuclear threats constitute a form of state crime—nuclear extortion—that is open to criminological analysis.

THE KOREAN WAR

The Backdrop of the Cold War

The United States, Great Britain, and the Soviet Union emerged from World War II as the major global powers. The Allies successfully defeated the imperialist designs of both Japan and Germany and soon established themselves as the political and economic architects of a new Europe. The February 1945 meeting of the Allies at Potsdam resulted in a plan to divide Europe into separate areas of occupation.

Germany was essentially divided into two occupation zones. The United States, Great Britain, and France occupied the west section of the country and the west section of Berlin, while the Soviets were given occupation rights of the Eastern portion of the country as well as the eastern portion of Berlin. The parceling of Germany was thought to be a temporary solution to the problem of rebuilding the physical, economic, political, and social structure of Germany. The temporary solution, however, became a permanent reality in the years to follow with the formation of two German countries: The eastern portion of Germany was established as the Soviet-influenced German Democratic Republic (GDR), and the area to the west became the Western-style capitalist state Federal Republic of Germany (FRG).

Outside of Germany, the geopolitics of the world also changed significantly. As a result of the war, the United States controlled or had great influence in Western Europe, the Philippines, Japan, and many other parts of the globe. An American empire was emerging (Chomsky, 1993; Gerson, 1995; Zinn, 1995). The Soviets controlled much of eastern Europe and created communist regimes in such countries as Yugoslavia, Rumania, and Poland. Thus, during the early stages of the Cold War, many battle lines were drawn between the West and East, pitting the antithetical political economies of capitalism and communism against one another.

After the war, the United States retained its close friendship with Great Britain. The Soviet Union, which incurred the most casualties of all the Allies in World War II, was increasingly viewed with suspicion by the West. During the war, President Truman was so skeptical of Stalin's plans for post-war Europe that he withheld the U.S. Manhattan Project from Stalin at the Yalta Conference. This distrust, whether well founded or not, was mutual.

Immediately after World War II, several events solidified the hostilities between the West and East. Soviet support of revolutionary movements in the Middle East, and of Iran in particular, was one such event. Prior to the Russian and U.S. entrance into World War II, the Allies had agreed to share oil rights in Iran. While the Western powers had withdrawn most of their forces in the region, the Soviets held their positions because they perceived inequity in the distribution of oil, claiming the West was reaping all the benefits. While the Soviets eventually withdrew from the region, primarily because they indeed got concessions from the West, they had demonstrated their resolve in Cold War economic and political posturing. In fact, Truman (1956) recalled that he seriously thought about bombing the Iranian-stationed Soviet troops with atomic weapons during the crisis, an emerging pattern for U.S. presidents.

Also adding to the conflict between the Soviets and the U.S. was the Berlin blockade. Since Berlin was approximately one hundred miles into East German territory, the West had historically used East German roads and railroads to administer the reconstruction of West Berlin. On June 24, 1948, Stalin instituted a blockade of all transportation routes to West Berlin with the intent of severing the West's ties to the city. While there is some evidence to suggest that the United States considered using atomic weapons in order to break the blockade, a decision was made to airlift supplies into West Berlin, thus avoiding another world war. Stalin eventually lifted the blockade in July 1949, but the rifts caused by the event reinforced already significant antagonisms.

Another important event in the early stages of the Cold War was the 1949 communist revolution in China. The United States had supported Chiang Kai-shek's fight against Mao's communist forces. Now that China had become communist, the United States was confronting another large country influenced by Marxist doctrine. The situation became exacerbated in 1950 with the signing of the Sino-Soviet Defense Treaty, which joined the Chinese and the Soviets against the West.

The relationship between the Soviet Union and the United States in the years immediately following World War II undoubtedly played a role in the United States' decision to intervene in the Korean conflict. Communism, personified in the political economies of the Soviet Union and its satellites, was perceived as the real enemy of the United States. In the U.S. view, the economic and political importance of protecting developing nations from the influence of communism, and thus protecting U.S. economic and political interests, soon began to dominate the military and political discourse. The military manifestations of the early Cold War period seldom found the United States and Soviet Union directly squaring off. It was in areas prone to influence by either country, areas such as Europe, Asia, and Southeast Asia, where the conflicts and interventions most often occurred. Perhaps no other statement confirms the underlying logic of the United States' concern during this period than the 1947 thoughts of Truman's Secretary of State Dean Acheson (1969, p. 219):

> Soviet pressure on the Straits, on Iran, and on northern Greece had brought the Balkans to the point where a highly possible Soviet breakthrough might open three continents to Soviet penetration. Like apples in a barrel infected by one rotten one, the corruption of Greece would affect Iran and all to the east. It would also carry infection to Africa through Asia minor and Egypt, and to Europe through Italy and France.

Political and Military Background of the Korean War

Communist North Korea, supported in purpose by both China and the Soviet Union, invaded South Korea on June 25, 1950. This invasion prompted a strong U.S. military response under the auspices of the United Nations. This was the first occasion of many in which the United States deployed massive ground troops to thwart communist aggression in Asia. While the intervention was formally conducted by the United Nations, the United States accounted for 85 percent of the armed forces supporting the South (Riggs and Plano, 1988). The war itself lasted only three years, but there is a substantial amount of evidence that the United States seriously considered the use of atomic weapons both during the war and also to enforce the 1953 Armistice. Moreover, both Presidents Truman and Eisenhower either overtly threatened or seriously considered the use of atomic weapons against the Chinese and North Koreans on a number of occasions. Most of these deliberations were conducted secretly in various private sessions with the Joint Chiefs of Staff, National Security Council, and other high-ranking executive officers. At other times, however, the considerations were made in public, obviously in an attempt to display U.S. resolve in the conflict.

Korea had been historically used by Russia and Japan as a strategic weapon for influence in Asia. As a result of a treaty signed in 1896, Korea was divided into North and South regions, with the Russians controlling the former and the Japanese controlling the area below the thirty-eighth parallel. Toward the end of World War II, as a result of the Soviet's declaration of war on Japan in late August 1945 and the U.S. atomic bombing of Hiroshima and Nagasaki that month, a formal agreement between the Soviet Union and the U.S. was reached: Japanese forces north of the thirty-eighth parallel would surrender to the Soviets, while Japanese forces south of the parallel would surrender to the United States. Ultimately this agreement turned North Korea into a Soviet satellite and South Korea into a quasi-occupied U.S. state. A cold war battle line was thus drawn in Korea.

While the United States vigorously supported the South Korean government led by Rhee, it was not entirely convinced of the strategic value of the region. Indeed, Truman felt that even during the early phases of the war, Korea was only of marginal importance to U.S. interests (Acheson, 1969). In 1946, the United States had sponsored, via the United Nations, free elections to be held in the South. Although aware of the political and economic instability of the region, the United States was more concerned about Western Europe and further Soviet influence in Germany. In fact there was nearly a complete U.S. withdrawal from Korea culminating in June 1949: South Korea was left with no tanks, airplanes, or other heavy artillery, and only a few rocket launchers, rifles, and small arms ammunition (Goulden, 1984). The Soviet Union, on the other hand, had a great deal of interest in North Korea. It installed a dedicated and faithful communist regime and deployed a significant amount of military personnel, artillery, ammunition, and weapons immediately following World War II.

The invasion of South Korea was assumed to be the product of the Soviet Union's desire to further establish communist authority in Asia. Although there is some degree of uncertainty on this issue, most U.S. policy makers seem to have subscribed to the theory that even if the invasion was not a direct product of Soviet imperialism, it was an indirect result of Soviet attempts at hegemony. Interestingly, Khrushchev (1970, p. 370) later denied that Stalin directly supported the invasion, but added that "Stalin did not try to dissuade. . . ."

The U.S. decision to commit itself militarily in Korea rests in part on the goals articulated in the Truman Doctrine, the famous foreign policy speech delivered before a joint session of Congress on March 12, 1947. Truman (1956, p. 106) remembered this speech as "a turning point in American foreign policy, which now declared that wherever aggression, direct or indirect, threatened the peace, the security of the United States was involved." The Truman Doctrine was primarily grounded in concerns over the political stability of Greece and Turkey, countries which played a key role in Cold War military posturing. While attempting to persuade Congress to grant funds to these struggling countries, the larger point of the address was to set the framework for supporting potentially friendly sovereigns, or politically unstable developing countries, for the purposes of U.S. influence and superiority across the globe. The president ended his address looking to the future.

> The seeds of totalitarian regimes are nurtured by misery and want. They spread and grow in the evil soul of poverty and strife. They reach their full growth when the hope of a people for a better life has died. We must keep that hope alive. If we falter in our leadership, we may endanger the peace of the world—and we shall surely endanger the welfare of our own nation. (Quoted in Lincoln, 1968, p. 20)

Less than three months after the announcement of the Truman Doctrine, Secretary of State George Marshall outlined a similar approach to the problem of Europe emphasizing the importance of economics. The Marshall Plan eventually set a more concrete basis for U.S. influence in Europe, and ultimately served, as evidenced by the Soviet rejection of the plan, as another instance in which Cold War lines were drawn. Thus, the Marshall Plan solidified Western influence in Western Europe, and at the same time forced the Soviets to structure their own economic vision of Eastern Europe.

The nature and form of U.S. foreign policy changed most dramatically as a result of the U.S. National Security Council study entitled NSC-68, submitted to Truman at a meeting on April 25, 1950. This study called for a significant increase in defense spending in order to confront the challenge and threat posed by the communists in general and the Soviet Union in particular. Secretary of State Dean Acheson (1969, p. 375), a primary drafter of the document, remembered,

> Our analysis of the (Soviet) threat combined the ideology of communist doctrine and the power of the Russian state into an aggressive expansionist drive, which found its chief opponent and, therefore, target in the antithetic ideas and power of our own country. . . . While our own society felt no compulsion to bring all societies in conformity with it, the Kremlin hierarchy was not content merely to entrench its regime but wished to expand its control directly and indirectly over other people within its reach.

In sum, NSC-68 pointed to the need of "containing" the Soviet Union by surrounding the country with both conventional and atomic weapons, a more specific but nevertheless generally consistent approach with the policy articulated in the Truman Doctrine. The report envisioned a 6,000-mile belt of nuclear bases spreading from northern Europe, through Middle East, across Southeast Asia, and extending into Japan and Korea. This led to the recommendation that an immense increase in atomic weapons research, design, and manufacture would be the most effective means of keeping the Soviets in check. In the report, atomic weapons were seen as playing a key role in the U.S. "policy of calculated and gradual coercion" (NSC-68).

As for NSC-68's impact on the decision to enter the Korean War, Acheson (1969) believed that the conflict put the theoretical and hypothetical scenarios of containment and thwarting communist expansionism into practice. And as Nitze admitted to Newhouse (1989, p. 82), the war "translated a think piece into an operational document." While fear of Soviet expansion and the need to "contain" communism, forcefully articulated in the Truman Doctrine and NSC-68, appear to be the driving force behind our involvement in Korea, the historian Howard Zinn (1995, p. 421) argues that the protection of empire was also key:

> So it was not just Soviet expansion that was threatening to the United States government and to American business interests. In fact, China, Korea, Indochina, the Philippines, represented local communist movements, not Russian fomentation. It was a general wave of anti-imperialist insurrection in the world, which would require gigantic American effort to defeat.

Status of Atomic Weapons during the Conflict

The Soviet Union first produced a nuclear reaction in December 1946, detonated its first atomic device in August 1949, and produced its first operable thermonuclear device in August 1953 (Cochran et al., 1984). Soviet nuclear weapons, however, were not fully deliverable until late 1955. The United States was well ahead of Soviet nuclear weapon capabilities, having at least 2 weapons in 1945, 9 in 1946, 13 in 1947, 50 in 1948, 250 in 1949, and 450 in 1950 (Cochran et al., 1984). While the United States certainly had the atomic advantage, both in megatonnage and numbers of weapons, the monopoly was soon viewed as questionable after the first Soviet atomic test in 1949 (see Table 3).

Table 3
United States and Soviet Union Atomic Stockpile during the Korean War

	United States	Soviet Union
1945	2	0
1946	9	0
1947	13	0
1948	50	0
1949	250	First atomic test
1950	450	0
1951	650	0
1952	1,000; first hydrogen bomb detonated	10–20
1953	1,350	<280; first hydrogen bomb detonated

The Soviets' first atomic test was a great surprise to the United States. Indeed, the estimates of Soviet atomic capabilities were predicted to be at least four to ten years away (Acheson, 1969; Powaski, 1987). Truman (1956) recalled that while he had expected the Soviets to test such a weapon sometime in the future, he was surprised that it had occurred so soon. Other accounts suggest that there was more anxiety over the Soviet test than Truman indicated; Acheson (1969, p. 345) recalled that the Soviet explosion "was the immediate cause of the review of our military and foreign policies." Powaski (1987) has argued that the general citizenry was shocked and frightened with the explosion, despite the administration's attempt to reassure the country; York (1976) found that Truman was so shaken that he required his informants to personally sign a document stating that they believed the Soviets had detonated the bomb.

One of the more significant effects of the Soviet test, in addition to buttressing the Truman Doctrine and NSC-68, was the U.S. decision to develop the hydrogen bomb. As early as the fall of 1949, Truman had considered developing the weapon, one with several times the explosive power of the fission atomic weapons currently in the U.S. stockpile. Two committees were charged to examine the problem: The General Advisory Committee (GAC) of the Atomic Energy Commission (AEC), comprised mostly of scientists, and a special committee of the National Security Counsel which included Secretary of State Acheson, Chair of the AEC David Lilienthal, and Secretary of Defense Louis Johnson (Powaski, 1987). In the end, the president concurred with the latter committee and approved production of the weapon. Truman's ultimate decision on the H-bomb was grounded in concerns over the Soviet Union's atomic program. In the final meeting on the subject, Lilienthal presented his reservations about the project but was interrupted by Truman who asked, "Can the Russians do it?" When all the participants responded affirmatively, Truman said, "In that case, we have no choice. We'll go ahead" (quoted in Powaski, 1987, p. 56).

By 1952 the conventional forces of the United States were rapidly rising along with a particular emphasis placed on the Air Force's role in the preparation of nuclear-ready airplanes and submarines. Quantitatively, the Soviet Union was still significantly behind in the atomic race. Despite the testing of a thermonuclear device in 1953, the weapon had only 20 percent of the explosive power of a comparable U.S. bomb (Clarfield and Wiecek, 1984). The Soviets had no nuclear-capable bombers until the 1955 production of the Bear A, while the United States had operationalized the nuclear-capable B-47 and B-52 bombers by 1952 (Clarfield and Wiecek, 1984). All told, U.S. defense spending quadrupled between the years of 1950 and

1953. When Eisenhower became president in 1953, the U.S. atomic stockpile approached 1350. At that time, aircraft were still relied on to deliver atomic weapons. It was not until the successful operationalization of the thermonuclear bomb in 1955 that ground-released intercontinental missiles entered official U.S. strategic policy.

Truman and Atomic Weapons in Korea

The June 25, 1950, North Korean invasion of South Korea prompted a quick response from the United Nations. While the Soviet delegation was not present, the other members of U.N. Security Council adopted a resolution calling for the withdrawal of North Korean forces below the thirty-eighth parallel. This resolution, adopted on the same day as the invasion, not only lamented and criticized the actions of North Korea, but also requested military support from all U.N. members to repel the attack. The United States accepted this offer on June 27, and ultimately provided the vast majority of military personnel and equipment.

On June 30 Truman ordered an embargo on all U.S. exports to Korea, a naval blockade of the entire Korean coast, and most importantly, aerial bombardments and ground-troop attacks of North Korean strongholds. After initially incurring significant losses, U.N. forces under the direction of General Douglas MacArthur crossed the thirty-eighth parallel into North Korea on October 9 and besieged the North Korean capital of Pyongyang. The result of this U.N. victory was that the West's troops maintained a highly threatening position on the Chinese mideastern border. Subsequently, the Chinese entered the war on November 27 and promptly forced U.S. troops beneath the thirty-eighth parallel. Now the United Nations (in actuality the United States) was fighting a second country and faced the uncomfortable position of risking a third world war.

Suddenly, a relatively small conflict began to appear as a more intensive and potentially explosive military situation.

The introduction of the Chinese into the civil war of Korea certainly raised the likelihood of an international war, pitting communist versus capitalist. With an estimated 200,000 Chinese ground soldiers in the war, the result was an enormous escalation of hostilities. Consideration of the use of atomic weapons then began to surface.

The first major possibility of the use of atomic weapons since World War II developed within the later stages of the Truman Administration. As early as July 1950, prior to the entrance of Chinese forces into the conflict, Truman ordered atomic bombs to be delivered to Great Britain. This marked the first time the United States allowed atomic bombs to be transferred across the Atlantic. Presumably this action was only symbolic, given that Truman (1956) believed the fighting in Korea would come to a close quickly, perceiving it to be a relatively minor conflict. But shortly after the Chinese entered the war, the question of the use of atomic weapons surfaced in a much more serious way.

Truman soon authorized a Joint Chiefs of Staff report ordering atomic bomb components to be stored on a warship patrolling the Mediterranean (Kaku and Axelrod, 1987). Furthermore, according to then–Secretary of State Dean Acheson (1969, p. 478), the Commandant of the U.S. Air Force College Orville Anderson announced at a speaking engagement that "the Air Force, equipped and ready, only awaited orders to drop its bombs on Moscow."

At a press conference on November 30, 1950, Truman asserted that "we will take whatever steps are necessary to meet the military solution." Furthermore, he answered the question of the possibility of using atomic weapons on the Chinese and North Koreans by stating, "That includes every weapon we have" and "There has always been active consideration of its use." When asked if the bomb would be used against civilian or military targets, Truman responded, "It's a matter the military people will have to decide" (Public Papers, 1950).

It is difficult to interpret these statements as overt threats to use atomic weapons against the Chinese and North Koreans. Indeed, immediately after Truman made these comments he added, "It is a terrible weapon, and it should not be used on innocent men, women and children who have nothing whatever to do with this military aggression. That happens when it is used" (Public Papers, 1950).

Several erroneous reports appeared in British and U.S. newspapers implying not only that was Truman prepared to use the bomb, but that General MacArthur, a vocal advocate for the weapon's use in Korea, had been given the power to personally order an atomic attack (Acheson, 1969). This prompted a visit from high-ranking British officers to confer with the president on the meaning of his statements. According to Acheson (1969) and Eisenhower (1963), the British were always more tentative about NATO use of nuclear weapons. At the meeting, the foreign delegation was briefed on the issue and were told that the use of atomic weapons was not actively being planned. Later that night, Truman released a press statement in an attempt to normalize the situation:

> Replies to the questions . . . do not represent any changes in this situation. Naturally there has been consideration of this subject since the outbreak of the hostilities in Korea, just as there is consideration of the use of all military weapons whenever our forces are in combat. However, it should be emphasized that, by law, only the President can authorize the use of the atomic bomb, and no such authorization has been given. (Quoted in Acheson, 1969, p. 479)

The extent to which Truman actively considered using atomic weapons is difficult to discern. Most of the evidence suggests that the atomic option was not popular among Truman's closest advisors. In an interview with Newhouse (1989, p. 83), Paul Nitze, director of the State Department's Policy Planning Group during the Korean War, confided that:

No one in the executive branch to my knowledge was pushing for the use of nuclear weapons. We were persuaded that the stockpile was too small to have allowed nuclear weapons to be used to any decisive effect against China, North Korea, or the Soviets in the event they entered the war.

Army Chief of Staff J. Lawton Collins, General Hoyt Vandenberg, and the remaining Chiefs of Staff decided against the use of the bomb on Korea and China for a number of reasons. Fear of a Soviet-Chinese conspiracy to divert U.S. atomic weapons to Korea in order to allow for an easier invasion of Europe, as well as lack of good targets were identified as important factors (Newhouse, 1989).

There were others in high military positions, however, who thought of the atomic option in Korea as viable. Stuart Symington, Chair of the National Security Board, Major General Orville Anderson, Commandant of the Air War College, and Secretary of the Navy Francis P. Matthews all called for a nuclear attack against China, and the possible targeting of the Soviet Union (Kaku and Axelrod, 1987). In fact, Matthews approved of the September 3, 1952, recommendation of the Deputy Assistant Secretary of State to spread the word on the possible U.S. use of nuclear weapons "so that it would get circulation in Korea and Japan, and China." This plan called for pamphlets to be dropped which read:

> The U.S. has consistently refused to accept prohibitions on the use of atomic weapons. . . . As the Presidential campaign grows, the pressure (to use them) will get much greater. The Government will probably not be able to resist it. There is one way to prevent the use of atomic weapons in Korea. This is to get an armistice without delay. (U.S. Department of State, 1984, p. 484)

While there is no evidence such a threat was carried out, it is clear that the nuclear weapons option was considered quite promising by many political and military officials. Truman himself, despite some of his public announcements to the contrary, evidently thought very seriously about using atomic weapons. In an entry in his personal diary on January 27, 1952, he wrote:

> It seems to me that the proper approach now would be an ultimatum with a ten day expiration limit, informing Moscow that we intend to blockade the China coast from the Korean border to Indo-China, and that we intend to destroy every military base in Manchuria. . . . This means all-out war. . . . It means Moscow, St. Petersburg, Mukden, Vladivostock, Peking, Shanghai, Port Arthur, Dairen, Odessa, Stalingrad, and every manufacturing plant in China and the Soviet Union will be eliminated, This is the final chance for the Soviet Government to decide whether it desires to survive or not. (Quoted in Kaku and Axelrod, 1987, p. 73)

There is no indication that Truman seriously discussed with others or actually planned to implement such a massive attack on China and the Soviet Union. His memoirs and other evidence support this interpretation. Publicly, at least, Truman also appeared keenly aware of the impact and import of the use of atomic weapons. In his final message on the state of the union, he asserted,

> The war of the future would be one in which man could extinguish millions of lives at one blow, demolish the great cities of the world, wipe out the cultural achievements of the past—and destroy the very structure of a civilization that has been slowly and painfully built up through hundreds of generations. Such a war is not a possible policy for rational men. (Public Papers, 1950, pp. 1124–25)

After all these considerations during the time of Truman's presidency, why were atomic weapons not used? Declassified documents reviewed by Kaku and Axelrod (1987), as well as a close reading of the discussions by the National Security Council, the Joint Chiefs of Staff, and other governmental officials, suggest that the principal reason was the fear of depleting the U.S. stockpile, rendering an atomic defense of Europe against a Soviet attack problematic.

It must be remembered that the Soviet Union was always viewed as the main threat. Indeed, Stalin had succeeded in establishing numerous satellite countries in Eastern Europe, contrary to his pledges of withdrawal at the 1945 Potsdam Conference. The United States' foreign policy was characterized by an extraordinary preoccupation with the security of Europe at this time. The primary threat at that point was the Soviet Union's perceived global imperialist aspirations. This ideology was officially codified in the top secret report "Shakedown," soon recognized as a contingency war plan by Truman. The basic thrust of the proposal was to respond to a Russian advance into Western Europe by an all-out nuclear attack on the Soviet Union.

This elaborate plan to completely destroy every major military and governmental installation in the Soviet Union was penned in 1949, a time in which the United States possessed only 250 weapons. The mission described in "Shakedown" required a first-day assault of over 100 weapons, plus several hundred secondary and contingency bombs. If this war plan was taken seriously by Truman, and by all indications it was, using the atomic bomb on North Korea and China would have significantly compromised the U.S. position vis-à-vis the Soviet Union. An atomic attack in Korea would, quite simply, have left the United States in a relatively vulnerable defensive posture in terms of atomic weapons, personnel, and delivery systems.

Truman left office in January 1953, a few weeks before Joseph Stalin died. The Korean War, however, was continuing and U.S. casualties were estimated at that time at 21,000 killed,

91,000 injured, and 13,000 missing (Eisenhower, 1963). Republican Dwight D. Eisenhower, who was on more than one occasion labeled the "peace candidate," had promised, if elected, to bring the war to a quick end. His strategy concerning the conflict was more combative, perhaps because of his military background, and clearly he was intolerant of the existing U.S. strategy in Korea. Truman had considered the atomic weapons option and ultimately found it wanting; under the Eisenhower administration, however, it would be a different story.

EISENHOWER'S ATOMIC STRATEGY IN KOREA

Eisenhower's public statements and private ideas concerning atomic weapons are somewhat enigmatic and often inconsistent. His farewell address to the nation in 1961, the famous speech warning against the dangers of the "military-industrial complex," and his "Atoms for Peace" plan delivered in 1953 to the U.N. General Assembly all indicate his sensitivity to the destructive effects of militarism and his hope for a peaceful world without the threat of global nuclear war. Eisenhower also reportedly shunned the use of atomic weapons in a meeting with Robert Cutler, his special assistant for national security: "You boys must be crazy. We can't use those awful things against Asians for the second time in less than ten years. My God" (quoted in Newhouse, 1989, p. 102).

In the spring after his election, Eisenhower (1963) reports having felt that there were three possible lines of action in Korea: (1) continue the war hoping for a quick armistice, (2) reinforce present troops and add more conventional forces, and (3) use atomic weapons to end the war quickly. He appeared to find the atomic option most attractive:

> To keep the attack from becoming costly, it was clear that
> we would have to use atomic weapons. This necessity was
> suggested to me by General MacArthur while I was presi-

dent elect. . . . The Joint Chiefs of Staff were pessimistic about the feasibility of using tactical atomic weapons on front-line positions; but such weapons would obviously be effective for strategic targets in North Korea, Manchuria, and on the Chinese coast. (p. 180)

Eisenhower felt that atomic weapons provided the most fruitful avenue for a U.S. victory in part because of his conviction that "it would be impossible for the United States to maintain the military commitments it now sustains did we not possess atomic weapons and the will to use them when necessary." Ever aware of British and French opposition to the use of atomic weapons on any occasion, Eisenhower thought that even if the use of such weapons on Korea and China occurred, "the rifts so caused could, in time, be repaired."

Eisenhower and his administration were also concerned about the Soviet Union's response to an atomic attack on China. Although China had yet to develop atomic weapons (thus representing a relatively minor threat), it was well known that the Soviets possessed several weapons (albeit not yet operational). Eisenhower also suspected that the Soviets were working on a hydrogen bomb.

Retrospectively, Eisenhower's contemplation of the use of atomic weapons can be understood by examining his general position on the nature of atomic weapons versus traditional weapons. He commented on October 30, 1953, some three months after the war's end, that "in the event of hostilities, the United States will consider nuclear weapons to be as available for use as other ammunition" (quoted in Newhouse, 1989, p. 91). In March 1955, he also indicated his support for the use of atomic weapons in any conflict: "In any combat where these things can be used on strictly military targets and for strictly military purposes, I see no reason why they shouldn't be used just exactly as you would use a bullet or anything else" (quoted in Newhouse, 1989, p. 91). Eisenhower also turned phrasemaker by referring to atomic weapons as a "Bigger Bang for the Buck," and began a policy of reliance on atomic weapons rather than conventional forces, known as the "New Look."

In the winter and spring of 1953, the advantages and disadvantages of using atomic weapons on North Korea and China were discussed at several secret meetings of the NSC and JCS. According to a National Security Council study released for deliberation on April 2, 1953, the major political advantages of using atomic weapons were identified as

1. the avoidance of a United Nations and United States "military disaster" in Korea;

2. a decisive end to the war which would make unnecessary continued military confrontations with China; and

3. a decisive end to the war which would make unnecessary a military confrontation with the Soviet Union. (U.S. Department of State, 1984, p. 846)

While it was perceived that there were numerous military and political advantages to using atomic weapons on Korea, the administration found many more political disadvantages. The NSC report identified these problems:

1. The disproportionality of destruction of Korea and China relative to military objectives in Korea;

2. Use of such weapons on Korea which would involve the West in general hostilities with Communist China;

3. Use of such weapons against China which would involve the West in hostilities with the Soviet Union; and

4. Use of such weapons which would lead to enemy retaliation in kind against vulnerable U.S.–U.N. targets.

The NSC report recommended that U.S. allies be consulted prior to the use of atomic weapons in order to avoid a political fallout. The council also advised the president to consider to what extent the political fallout from other "free nations" might dissipate support for the general objectives of the United States in Korea.

Eisenhower communicated his concern about the possible backlash from using atomic weapons in several meetings. In the January 8, 1954, meeting of the National Security Council, where possible courses of action were discussed if the truce were broken, he asserted that "our people have understood the atomic weapon, but we must be a little more patient with our allies, who had not fully grasped the import of atomic weapons" (U.S. Department of State, 1984, p. 1704).

At a December 10, 1953, meeting of the NSC, Eisenhower was deeply concerned about Secretary of State Dulles's report of his meeting with British Prime Minister Churchill. Dulles disclosed that Churchill believed "there would be a world-wide revulsion" to the use of atomic weapons (U.S. Department of State, 1984, p. 1654). Also at that meeting, Eisenhower recalled agreeing with Churchill's earlier recommendation that he avoid suggesting in his address to the United Nations that the United States was considering using the atomic bomb. Eisenhower had not mentioned the plans in his December 8 "Atoms for Peace" speech. On January 8, 1954, during a National Security Council meeting, Eisenhower again brought up his concerns with reactions to the use of atomic weapons if North Korea violated the truce: "The real problem was how to get public opinion in the free world to grasp the fact that the Communists did renew their aggression" (p. 1705).

There is little doubt that Eisenhower and his administration seriously considered world opinion in their deliberations over the use of the bomb. It is clear that the global social reaction to its use was anticipated to be negative and potentially damaging to the United States. Perhaps this explains Eisenhower's concern for changing the perception of atomic weapons.

On February 11, 1953, at a NSC meeting that included all of

Eisenhower's key military and political advisors, serious consideration on the use of tactical nuclear weapons on North Korean strongholds surfaced. While there was some disagreement, Dulles and Eisenhower eventually came to the conclusion that, as a general policy, atomic weapons should not be distinguished from conventional weapons. The minutes of the meeting read,

> Secretary Dulles discussed the moral problem and the inhibition on the use of the A-bomb, and Soviet success to date in setting these weapons apart from all other weapons as being in a special category. It was his opinion that we should try to break down this false distinction. (U.S. Department of State, 1984, p. 770)

After this statement, Eisenhower indicated his agreement, stated that perhaps U.S. allies should be consulted on the issue, and even suggested that the allies should be requested to supply more conventional military personnel and equipment if they refused to consider the atomic option. According to the minutes of the meeting, Eisenhower ultimately concluded that he would not make that demand on the British.

The subject again took center stage in a March 31, 1953, discussion of the National Security Council. The minutes of the meeting state:

> Mr. (Deane) Malott (special civilian advisor to the president) argues that he nevertheless believed that we ought to use a couple of atomic bombs in Korea. The President replied that perhaps we should, but we could not blind ourselves to the effects of such a move on our allies, which would be very serious since they feel that they will be the battleground in an atomic war between the United States and the Soviet Union. Nevertheless, the President and Secretary Dulles were in complete agreement that somehow or another the tabu which surrounds the use of atomic

weapons would have to be destroyed. While Secretary Dulles admitted that in the present state of world opinion we could not use an A-bomb, we should make every effort now to dissipate this feeling. (U.S. Department of State, 1984, p. 825)

On May 20, 1953, Eisenhower further discussed how the atomic weapon could be normalized:

It was the President's view that we ought to at once to [sic] begin to infiltrate these ideas into the minds of our allies. If the ground were prepared and the seeds were planted in a quiet and informal way, there was a much better chance of acceptance than if we suddenly confronted the allied governments with a full-fledged plan to end the war by military decision. There was general agreement with the President's point. . . . Secretary Smith reemphasized his views . . . that a quick victory would go far to sell our allies on even the most drastic course of action in Korea. (U.S. Department of State, 1984, p. 1066)

Thus, not only did the Eisenhower administration consider the possible social and political reactions to the use of atomic bombs in Korea important in its deliberations, but also it believed that attempts should be made to normalize the atomic bomb into the category of conventional weaponry. Indeed, it appears as though the administration operated under the assumption that atomic weapons should be regarded as quantitatively, not qualitatively, distinct from conventional weapons.

Several meetings were scheduled in the winter and spring to consider the question of targets. By March, as Chair of the Joint Chiefs of Staff General Omar Bradley recalled,

the JCS took the unprecedented step of recommending that the "timely use of atomic weapons should be considered against military targets affecting operations in Korea" and "planned as an adjunct possible military course of action involving direct action against Communists China and Manchuria. . . ." In the meantime, Ike had independently reached the decision the JCS were now voicing: if necessary, use atomic weapons in Korea. (Quoted in Kaku and Axelrod, 1987, p. 81)

All of the evidence, both primary and secondary, points to Eisenhower's serious consideration and actual targeting of U.S. atomic weapons. There is no question that the use of atomic weapons was viewed as an acceptable method of ending the hostilities in Korea. Indeed, of the six courses of action outlined by the Joint Chiefs of Staff and the National Security Council during the latter parts of the war, four were considered possible only if they were implemented with the aid of atomic weapons drops on Korea and China.

The strongest evidence that an atomic threat was made against North Korea and China is found in Eisenhower's (1963, p. 181) memoirs:

The lack of progress in long-stalemated talks . . . demanded definite measures on our part to put an end to these intolerable conditions. One possibility was to let the Communist authorities understand that, in the absence of satisfactory progress, we intended to move decisively without inhibition in our use of weapons, and would no longer be responsible for confining hostilities to the Korean Peninsula. We would not be limited by any world-wide gentleman's agreement. In India and in the Formosa Straits area, and the truce negotiations at Panmunjon, we dropped the word, discreetly, of our intention. We felt quite sure it would reach Soviet and Chinese Communist ears. Soon the prospects for armistice negotiations seemed to improve.

Adding further validity to the existence of the threats, Eisenhower claimed later in his presidency:

I let it be known that if there was not going to be an armistice . . . we were not going to be bound by the kinds of weapons that we would use. . . . I don't mean to say that we'd have used those great big things and destroyed cities, but we would use them enough to win. (Quoted in Lens, 1982, p. 43)

The next threat was carried out by Secretary of State Dulles on a visit to India on May 20, 1953. At a meeting with Indian Prime Minister Jawaharal Nehru, Dulles, according to his notes, dropped the word that "if the armistice negotiations collapsed, the United States would probably make a stronger rather than a lesser military exertion, and that this might well extend the area of conflict" (quoted in Adams, 1961, p. 34). Later, Dulles admitted to Berding (1965, p. 129) that the intent of the meeting was to make clear our "intention to wipe out the industrial complex in Manchuria if we did not get an armistice." The message was transferred from India, probably through the Ambassador to China, to Bejing. Eisenhower was very careful not to make such an atomic threat directly to the Chinese. The Chinese, however, were very much aware of the threat made by Dulles, as well as the earlier threat by Eisenhower's negotiators at Panmunjon (Eisenhower, 1963).

Obviously, the threats were not carried out. On July 27, 1953, a truce was signed between the United Nations and North Korea. The question of whether the atomic threats were instrumental in ending the war is not easily answerable. According to Eisenhower, Nixon, and many other top decision makers, the threat of an atomic attack ended the war. In spite of this informed hypothesis, one cannot ignore the fact that the Chinese continued to attack U.S. forces after the threat; in addition, and perhaps more importantly, the death of Joseph Stalin might have been a significant variable in ending the war as well. Nevertheless, it is important to note that both the Eisenhower and Truman administrations actively considered using atomic weapons during the three year conflict; while Truman discarded the idea of an atomic bombing of Korea rather quickly, Eisenhower saw atomic diplomacy as an effective way to end the war.

ANALYSIS

The most obvious answer to the question of why the illegal threat to use atomic weapons occurred in Korea is that Eisenhower and his administration wanted to end the Korean War and they were under considerable pressure to do so. During his presidential campaign, Eisenhower had pledged to resolve the Korean situation and his administration felt strong pressures to achieve that goal. Eisenhower was frustrated by the stalemate in negotiations and searched for a way to resolve the conflict quickly.

In addition to the administration's goal, the broader structural and ideological forces that had lead the United States into the war in the first place also influenced the decision. The Cold War political and ideological struggle with communism that brought the United States to Korea dictated that the war had to be ended on terms most favorable to the United States as possible. The containment of communist expansion, and the implications that it had for the protection of U.S. allies and America's own national security, was the reason most forcefully articulated by both the Truman and Eisenhower administrations.

But Korea was not just a war fought to protect the United States and its allies from communist aggression. Korea was also a war to defend American spheres of influence and protect U.S. economic and political interests. As Zinn (1995) has pointed out, it was a war fought to stem a wave of anti-imperialist Third World insurrections against the American empire, whether they were fomented by Moscow or not.

The availability of atomic weapons, the experience of their

dramatic effect in ending World War II, and the rational instrumental logic characteristic of most organizational structures led the Eisenhower administration to consider the use of atomic bombs as the most effective and efficient means to end the war. The anticipated negative allied reaction to the use of atomic bombs, however, discouraged the administration from choosing that option. In this regard, it is interesting to note Eisenhower's attempt to "normalize" atomic weapons and convince the British, in particular, that these weapons were no different from conventional weapons, only a bit more powerful. Concern about overextending atomic resources in Asia at the expense of the defense of Western Europe also played a role in the decision not to use atomic weapons in Korea at that time.

The next best option open to the Eisenhower administration was to *threaten* to use atomic weapons to end the war. The secret nature of the threat reduced the possibility of negative reaction from the world community, and yet was real enough, in the shadow of Hiroshima and Nagasaki, to be effective with the communists. Whether the threat to use atomic weapons in Korea was ultimately responsible for bringing an end to the war, no one knows for sure. But it is clear that at least one important person thought the threat had worked, and that would lead to the same threat being employed again in the next decade.

4

The Threat to Use Nuclear
Weapons in Vietnam

Just as it did during the Korean
War, the United States also threatened to use weapons of mass
destruction in Vietnam. While there are some similarities between these two threats, there are significant differences as well.

THE VIETNAM WAR

Before addressing President Nixon's threat to use nuclear
weapons in Vietnam, we examine the historical context of the
Vietnam War, including the influence of the Cold War and the
political and military situation in Vietnam, as well as the Johnson administration's position toward nuclear weapons.

The Cold War between 1953 and 1965

Antagonistic relations between the Soviet Union and the
United States continued after the Korean War. The Eisenhower
administration maintained the policy of containment. Although the United States did not commit itself to any particular
region to the same degree it did in Korea, it did engage in economic, political, and low-intensity wars in a variety of areas
around the world in an effort to protect empire and advance
its political and economic interests.

The area in which the United States held the most interest immediately following the Korean War was Southeast Asia. The United States had supported the French occupation of Vietnam since 1950. Between the years of 1950 and 1954, the United States funneled over $1.2 billion to the French, accounting for nearly 70 percent of cost of the occupation (LaFeber, 1991). The U.S. commitment to this region became even more significant in 1954 when funds were given directly to the newly created government of South Vietnam. By 1955, the French were gone and the United States installed Ngo Dinh Diem as president of South Vietnam. Heavy U.S. commitment in this region would continue until 1973.

Outside of Southeast Asia, the United States also applied its policy of containment, again due to the fear of communist expansion. Of particular importance was the policy designed by the Eisenhower administration, eventually labeled the "Eisenhower Doctrine," which held that the United States would support any Middle Eastern country threatened by communism. In part, U.S. involvement in the brief Suez Crisis of 1956 can be viewed as an application of this policy. More indicative of the policy, however, was the direct military involvement of the United States in the 1958 Lebanon Crisis, when 14,000 U.S. troops landed on Lebanese soil to support the government of President Chamoun. Although the Lebanese conflict was in real terms a civil war, the Eisenhower administration nonetheless applied the policy of containment to the region, attempting to both deter Soviet expansion into the area and prevent instability in remaining pro-Western Arab countries (Blechman and Kaplan, 1978). Indeed, during the mid to late 1950s, the Middle East was viewed by the United States as susceptible to communist infiltration, especially because of Egyptian President Nasser's apparent sympathy for communism and his more than casual association with the Soviet Union.

In relative terms, Germany and Berlin had become somewhat stable since the 1948 Soviet Blockade. However, in the late 1950s and early 1960s, Berlin and Germany once again became principal maneuvering areas of the Cold War. On November 10, 1958, Soviet Premier Khrushchev demanded Western surrender of West Berlin. Predictably, Western reaction to this demand was hostile. Khrushchev then hinted at the possibility of using "the greatest possible force" to enforce the proposal (Slusser, 1978, p. 357). The Soviet premier set a deadline of six months for the completion of negotiations on the question. For the next ten months, the United States and Soviet Union played a miniature war game by blocking roads and refusing passage to one another in various sections of Berlin. However, it wasn't long before the crisis came to a halt, and by September 1959, the Soviets, wishing to avoid any major military action, withdrew their demands. This battle in the Cold War ended where it began. Two years later the question of Berlin and the two Germanys again took center stage when Khrushchev made similar demands on the Kennedy administration to allow the reunification of the entire city of Berlin with the communist East. The confrontation resulted in the construction of the Berlin Wall and the famous "Checkpoint Charlie" tank confrontation.

While Western Europe, the two Germanys, and the divided city of Berlin were major sources of confrontation during this period of the Cold War, it was in 1961 and 1962 that the United States became involved in two of the most dangerous clashes between the Korean and Vietnam Wars: The attempted invasion of Cuba and the Cuban Missile Crisis. These two incidents represent the general geographic movement of the Cold War from direct confrontation in Europe to peripheral but nonetheless important areas of the globe.

On New Year's Day, 1959, the small island of Cuba, located some ninety miles from southern Florida, came under the leadership of the revolutionary communist Fidel Castro. Both the Eisenhower and Kennedy administrations feared such a close geographic relationship with a Soviet-supported government.

The U.S. Central Intelligence Agency provided military training and equipment to revolutionary Cuban exiles, and promised air support for a coup d'état of the Castro regime. The Bay of Pigs invasion, fully supported and designed under both Eisenhower and Kennedy, failed miserably, with the Cuban revolutionaries sustaining total defeat, principally because of the U.S. decision to not supply the promised air support.

The last major confrontation between the Soviet Union and United States prior to the U.S. entrance in the Vietnam War was the Cuban Missile Crisis, which again demonstrated the United States' concern with Soviet influence in areas outside of Eastern Europe. In October 1962, the United States became aware of the construction of Soviet nuclear missile bases on Cuban soil and instituted a thirteen-day blockade of Soviet ships suspected of transporting nuclear weapon materials. Within two weeks of the blockade, the Soviet ships turned back to the Atlantic with the agreement that the United States would not attempt to reinvade Cuba and that it would evacuate some of its nuclear missile sites in eastern Turkey. Despite both sides considering the outcome beneficial, the antagonisms between the United States and Soviet Union were not reduced or diminished in intensity.

The Kennedy and Johnson administrations maintained policies of containment consistent with those of the earlier administrations of Eisenhower and Truman. Indeed, President Kennedy applied this logic to Cuba and other areas of U.S. interest:

it is clear that the forces of communism are not to be underestimated, in Cuba or anywhere else in the world . . . it is clear that this Nation, in concert with all the free nations of this hemisphere, must take an even closer and more realistic look at the menace of external Communist intervention and domination in Cuba . . . it is clearer than ever that we face a relentless struggle in every corner of the globe that goes far beyond the clash of armies or even nuclear armaments. The armies are there. . . . The nuclear armaments are there. But they serve primarily as the shield behind which subversion, infiltration, and a host of other tactics steadily advance. (Quoted in Lincoln, 1968, p. 133)

The Cold War continued throughout the post–Korean War era. A series of crises erupted every few years which manifested the deep animosity between the two superpowers. The only real thawing of the Cold War occurred during the period of detente in the late 1960s and early 1970s. The 1968 Strategic Arms Limitation Talks (SALT), and the successful Nixon administration policy of forcing competition between the Soviets and Chinese, helped to lessen international tensions during this period.

U.S. policies, though undergoing slight revisions in different presidential administrations, nevertheless maintained a commitment to thwart communist expansion via low-intensity war. While Cuba and Germany did not escalate into full military confrontations between the superpowers, the small country of Vietnam, which measures less in size than the state of California, proved to be the region where the Cold War would turn hot again. Much like the U.S. entrance into the Korean War in 1950, U.S. intervention in Vietnam was a reflection of the containment policy.

Political and Military Background of the Vietnam War

Vietnam represents the cornerstone of the Free World in Southeast Asia, the keystone to the arch, the finger in the dike. . . . Her economy is essential to the economy of all of Southeast Asia. (President Kennedy, quoted in Lafeber, 1991, p. 232)

In the modern era, Vietnam has never experienced a prolonged period of peace. Controlled by the Chinese until the early fifteenth century, the country was first granted independence in 1428. However, the French invasion in 1861 further established the region as a colony, despite numerous clashes between the indigenous peoples of the area and the French occupying forces. It was not until the defeat of the French in 1954 that the country of Vietnam gained any degree of sovereignty.

In July 1954, as a result of negotiations in Geneva, Vietnam was divided into two sovereigns, North and South. The United States, Britain, the Soviet Union, and France designed the plan along with representatives of the north and south regions of Vietnam. In what was thought to be a temporary solution to the problems of the country, the areas of North and South were demarcated at the seventeenth parallel. The Geneva negotiators agreed to the creation of a communist-led North Vietnamese government, and a pro-Western South government.

The United States soon became the major supporter of the government of South Vietnam, led by the brutal anticommunist Ngo Dinh Diem, who ruled until his U.S.–supported assassination in 1963. The United States provided military advisors, ground troops, and other personnel and equipment to the South Vietnamese until its exit from the war in 1973. By 1963, the United States funneled over $500 million in aid and provided nearly 15,000 military personnel to the Diem administration (Karnow, 1983). In the North, the government was led by Ho Chi Minh, who received significant support from the Soviet Union and China.

Between 1954 and 1965, the two Vietnams were engaged in constant low-intensity warfare. The North Vietnamese, inspired by a nationalist ideology calling for a return to a united Vietnam, increasingly stepped up attacks on bordering cities and chief military and political areas in the South. South Vietnam, too, engaged in offensive attacks against the North, with a comparable level of violence directed toward communist sympathizers and dissenters in both areas of the region.

The United States committed itself to Indochina, and particularly Vietnam, in the post–World War II era. Containment and the protection of economic interests guided U.S. actions in the region. As early as 1952, when the United States was in the midst of the Korean War, the National Security Council had formed its objectives on Southeast Asia: "To prevent the countries of Southeast Asia from passing into the communist orbit, and to assist them to develop will and ability to resist communism from within and without and to contribute to the strengthening of the free world" (Pentagon Papers, 1971, p. 27).

In the same secret memo, the NSC also pointed to the chain of U.S. military bases throughout the Pacific: "Control of all of Southeast Asia would render the U.S. position in the Pacific offshore island chain precarious and would seriously jeopardize fundamental U.S. security interests in the Far East." The memo went on to note, "Southeast Asia, especially Malaya and Indonesia, is the principal world source of natural rubber and tin, and a producer of petroleum and other strategically important commodities." Thus, the concerns of empire were also important here (Zinn, 1995).

The council also recommended continued and complete support of the French occupying forces, as well as contingency plans for air strikes and ground-troop deployment should the French come under Chinese attack, and an assortment of "aggressive military, political, and psychological program(s) to defeat or seriously reduce the Viet Minh forces" (Pentagon Papers, 1971, vol. 1, p. 30). President Kennedy continued Eisenhower's policy of gradual escalation in Vietnam less than five months after taking office. In a proposal offered by an interdepartmental task force, Kennedy approved the following measures: Expanded "intelligence, unconventional warfare, and political-psychological activities," penetration of North Vietnamese communication systems, enlarged Central Intelligence Agency training for South Vietnamese nationals, and enhanced propaganda techniques to include the "testimony of rehabilitated prisoners, stressing the errors of Communism . . . broadcast to Communist held areas, including North Vietnam, to induce defections" (Pentagon Papers, 1971, p. 120).

U.S. escalation of the war came in August 1964, when the destroyer *Maddox* presumably was attacked by North Vietnamese patrol boats in the Gulf of Tonkin, a small body of water adjacent to the Chinese–North Vietnamese border (whether this attack actually took place has been vigorously debated). This incident provided legislative cover for the escalation already being planned. On August 5, President Johnson requested that Congress allow him to take "any measures necessary to repel any armed attack against the United States and to prevent further aggression" (quoted in Lincoln, 1968, p. 294). The permission was given by Congress two days later in the form of the Tonkin Gulf Resolution.

President Johnson ordered the first bombing campaign of North Vietnam, code-named Rolling Thunder, in early 1965 and committed more than 200,000 troops to the region by December of that year (Karnow, 1983). Under the Johnson Administration, the policy employed was one of "gradual escalation," whereby it was hypothesized that small quantities of ground troops and air attacks would lead to larger-scale attacks and ultimately U.S. victory. In large part, this policy was enacted to protect the secrecy of the U.S. bombing missions and to attempt to confine the hostilities within Indochina.

It is important to note the general U.S. commitment during the war. By the end of the war in 1973, the United States had dropped over seven and one-half million tons of bombs on both North and South Vietnamese soil; committed 500,000 soldiers; employed over 400,000 tons of napalm to deforest suspected Vietcong strongholds; lost over 50,000 soldiers; and had invested $150 billion in the effort (Harrison, 1982; Lens, 1982).*

---

*Unlike the battle lines in the Korean War, in which the thirty-eighth

In 1973, the United States finally withdrew from the conflict. South Vietnam's President Nguyen Van Thieu pleaded with the West to maintain its commitment in the area, but in the United States widespread disapproval of the war and continued failure in suppressing Vietcong influence ultimately forced the decision to withdraw (Nixon, 1978). The United States lost more than 50,000 soldiers (the third deadliest war of the U.S.) and had been solidly defeated by a less technologically developed Third World country. All U.S. troops had evacuated Vietnam by March 1973 (Harrison, 1982).

The U.S. withdrawal did not cease the fighting in Vietnam. Northern forces ultimately took control of the entire country with the capture of the South Vietnam capital of Saigon on April 30, 1975. Vietnam was no longer divided into North and South. For the first time, U.S. containment policy had failed.

Status of Nuclear Weapons during the Vietnam War

The qualitative and quantitative expansion of nuclear weapons immediately following the Korean War made the situation faced by the United States and Soviet Union during the Vietnam War much more precarious. While Great Britain, France, and China also maintained a nuclear stockpile by 1965, the former two countries' weapons were largely under the control of the North Atlantic Treaty Organization (NATO) alliance, while Chinese nuclear weapons remained primitive in comparison to U.S. and Soviet stockpiles. With the nuclearization of Western Europe by NATO in 1954, and the Soviet stationing of nuclear delivery systems and warheads both within their country and in sections of the Baltic states, the Cold War progressively revolved around the ability to deter and threaten the use of nuclear weapons to maintain "security." This is in sharp

---

parallel clearly designated communist versus capitalist regions, North Vietnamese troops were scattered throughout both North and South Vietnam, as well as Cambodia. Thus, the United States expanded the bombing zones to include the geographic areas it was ostensibly protecting.

contrast to the military situation during the Korean War when both the United States and the Soviets depended mostly on conventional arms.

Table 4 illustrates the nuclear weapons stockpiles of the United States and the Soviet Union from the end of the Korean

Table 4
U.S. and Soviet Nuclear Weapons Stockpiles: 1955–1973

Year	United States	Soviet Union
1955	2,760	280
1956	4,000	900
1957	5,800	1,590
1958	8,190	2,440
1959	13,000	3,550
1960	18,900	4,520
1961	23,300	5,770
1962	26,700	7,180
1963	29,000	8,970
1964	31,100	10,600
1965	32,400	12,300
1966	33,000	13,700
1967	32,800	15,500
1968	31,300	17,400
1969	29,100	19,000
1970	27,000	20,800
1971	26,700	22,100
1972	27,500	23,600
1973	28,700	25,400

Source: Cochran, Arkin, and Hoenig (1984).

War through the Vietnam War. Although the United States has always maintained the lead in pure numbers of nuclear weapons, if one takes into account the actual megatonnage of weapons until 1967, there is near parity. But in the years from 1967 to the present, the Soviet Union has possessed the advantage in pure destruction capacity. From 1969 to the mid 1980s, the Soviet Union maintained at least twice the amount of total megatonnage of the United States; in the years between 1972 and 1980, Soviet megatonnage was three times more powerful than U.S. destructive capabilities (see Cochran et al., 1984). The noticeable difference between actual weapons and megatonnage is explained by the Soviet's tendency to build high-yield intercontinental ballistic missiles (ICBMs) and submarine-launched ballistic missiles (SLBMs), and the U.S. strategy of making more weapons with lower yields.

Comparing the bombing of Hiroshima with the destructive capabilities of U.S. nuclear weapons during the Vietnam period, one realizes the astounding pace of development of nuclear weapons technology. The 12 kiloton (12,000 tons) bomb dropped on Hiroshima is estimated to have killed at least 130,000 people (Perkins, 1991). The United States had stockpiled 2,000 megatons (2 million tons) by the end of the Korean War, and 10,900 megatons (11 million tons) at the start of the Vietnam War. If the United States had detonated all of its nuclear weapons during the Vietnam War era, the destructive capacity would be enough to kill the world's population some thirty-five times over (Perkins, 1991).

U.S nuclear weapons policy has always been based on the concept of deterrence. This doctrine holds that a Soviet invasion of Western Europe or another pro-Western region would be deterred if the aggressor understood that the United States would respond to such an invasion with nuclear forces. This strategy, known as the "first-use option," has been official NATO policy since 1967. Additionally, the policy of deterrence was hypothesized, especially during the 1950s and 1960s under the "mutual assured destruction" (MAD) doctrine, to prevent any Soviet or U.S. first strike of homelands, since such a strike would be guaranteed to provoke equally damaging attacks on the country that first used nuclear weapons. While U.S. deterrence policy has undergone minor changes throughout the nuclear age, the theory most popular during the period of the Vietnam War was "flexible response," which, in congruence with the "first-strike" policy of earlier years, held that any region threatened with Soviet occupation or invasion would be assisted by U.S. nuclear forces.

Johnson and Nuclear Weapons Considerations

President Johnson inherited the complicated situation in Vietnam fully aware of most U.S. covert operations in the region. His views on the importance of U.S. influence in the area again exemplifies the doctrine of containment. In a series of interviews with Doris Kearns (1973, p. 316) Johnson recalled his position:

> The Communists' desire to conquer the world is just like the lawyer's desire to be the ultimate judge on the Supreme Court or the politician's desire to be President. You see, the Communists want to rule the world, and if we don't stand up to them, they will do it. And we'll be slaves.

In the same interview Johnson very bluntly professed his belief in the domino theory:

> So I knew that if the aggression succeeded in South Vietnam, then the aggressors would simply keep on going until all of Southeast Asia fell into their hands. . . . Now I know these academics thought all they had to do was to write a lot of words proclaiming the death of the domino theory and their words alone could make the Communist threat vanish overnight. But while the impotent academics were talking, Moscow and Peking would be moving to extend

their control and soon we would be fighting in Berlin or elsewhere, and so would begin World War III. (Kearns, 1973, p. 330)

The question of the use or threat to use nuclear weapons during the Johnson administration manifested itself on a number of occasions. While there was considerably less discussion about the issue than in the Eisenhower or Truman administrations, Johnson's advisors did examine the possibility. Prior to full U.S. involvement in Vietnam, South Vietnamese General Nguyen Khanh and U.S. Secretary of State Dean Rusk met in May 1964 to discuss the possibility of a U.S. intervention. With Khanh delighted at the prospect, Rusk delineated President Johnson's major concerns in the event of full-scale intervention: "The U.S. would never again get involved in a land war in Asia limited to conventional forces. Our population was 190,000,000. Mainland China had at least 700,000,000. We would not allow ourselves to be bled white fighting them with conventional weapons" (Pentagon Papers, 1973, vol. 2, p. 322).

Rusk continued, this time emphasizing the likelihood of using nuclear weapons:

This meant that if the escalation brought about a major Chinese attack, it would also involve the use of nuclear arms. Many free world leaders would oppose this. Many Asians seemed to see an element of racial discrimination in the use of nuclear arms; something we would do to Asians but not to Westerners. (Pentagon Papers, vol. 2, 1973, p. 322)

Khanh replied he "certainly had no quarrel with American use of nuclear arms . . . if the Chinese used masses of humanity, we would use superior firepower."

This meeting was probably based, at least in part, on the discussions that took place a month earlier in a National Security Council meeting in April 1964. According to the minutes of the meeting, the discussion on whether to bomb North Vietnam into submission flirted with the nuclear option:

> There was speculation about whether the use of nuclear weapons against North Vietnam would bring in the Russians. Rusk had been impressed, so he said, by Chiang Kai-shek's recent, strongly expressed opposition to any use by the United States of nuclear weapons. . . . Bundy conjectured for argument's sake that nukes used in wholly unpopulated areas solely for the purposes of interdiction might have a different significance than if used otherwise. It is not reported that any examination of effectiveness . . . was essayed. (Pentagon Papers, 1973, vol. 3, p. 65)

At the U.S.–sponsored Honolulu conference in June 1964, top military and political officials discussed further plans of action against North Vietnam. When debating the possibility of conventional versus nuclear campaigns, Secretary of Defense McNamara noted that all the planning thus far was on the basis that a Soviet or Chinese reaction to an attack on North Vietnam was likely only if such attacks were massive (Pentagon Papers, 1973). He argued that in order to ensure that the larger communist nations would not get involved, the first stages of attacks should be limited. He noted, however, that it was essential to make contingency plans in the event of the expansion of belligerents. According to the minutes of the meeting, the nuclear weapons issues then took center stage:

> McNamara then went on to say that the possibility of a major ground action also led to a serious question of having to use nuclear weapons at some point. Admiral Felt responded emphatically that there was no possible way to hold off the communists on the ground without the use of tactical nuclear weapons, and that it was essential that the commanders be given the freedom to use these as it had been assumed under the various plans. He said that with-

out nuclear weapons, the ground force requirement was and had always been completely out of reach. (Pentagon Papers, 1973, vol. 3, p. 175)

There is also mention of the possible use of nuclear weapons in the November 1964 National Security Council Working Group paper "Courses of Action, Southeast Asia." This report, submitted to the Joint Chiefs of Staff for analysis, acknowledged the fact that a full military commitment to the region

would involve high risks of a major conflict in Asia, which could not be confined to air and naval action but would almost inevitably involve a Korean-scale ground action and possibly even the use of nuclear weapons at some point. (Pentagon Papers, 1973, vol. 3, p. 623)

The Joint Chiefs responded critically to the analogy of Korea and replied to the nuclear weapons hypothesis by stating that the phrase " 'Possibly even the use of nuclear weapons at some point' is of course why we spend billions to have them. If China chooses to go to war against us she has to contemplate their possible use, just as anyone else" (Pentagon Papers, 1973, vol. 3, p. 623).

It would be erroneous to conclude that there were not serious doubts about the use of nuclear weapons on the North Vietnamese in the period prior to full U.S. military intervention. If we survey the opinions of the more powerful advisors such as McNamara, Rusk, and Bundy during this time, there appears to be a consensus that, if employed, they could be successful only if used sparingly, or "to hold off an enemy to save a force threatened with destruction, or to knock out a special target" (Pentagon Papers, 1973, vol. 3, p. 631). A strategy that included major roles for nuclear weapons simply did not exist at this time.

This does not mean that there were not several advisors to the president who saw the value of nuclear weapons in the region. In his autobiography, the commander of U.S. forces in Vietnam, General William Westmoreland (1980, p. 91), criticized the Johnson administration for not using them:

> If Washington officials were so intent on sending a message to Hanoi, surely small tactical nuclear weapons would be a way to tell Hanoi something, as two atomic bombs had spoken convincingly to Japanese officials during World War II, and the threat of atomic bombs induced the North Koreans to accept meaningful negotiations during the Korean War. It could be that the use of a few small tactical nuclear weapons in Vietnam—or even the threat of them—might have quickly brought the war there to an end.

Despite Westmoreland's position, which paralleled that of a few other important advisors of the president, Johnson had difficulty accepting the argument. To understand this, it is important to note the strain Johnson experienced during the bombing campaigns against North Vietnam. While some of his military advisors recommended significantly increased forces and attacks against Vietcong strongholds, Johnson was at first reluctant to expand the conflict. One of his greatest fears was that excessive bombing could trigger Soviet or Chinese entrance into the hostilities. One should not underestimate the importance of this concern, since Johnson enacted moratoriums on bombings several times during the war in an attempt to end the war politically.* Johnson outlined his theory to Kearns (1973, p. 264):

> I saw our bombs as my political resources for negotiating a peace . . . our bombs could be used as sticks against the

---

*In a December 11, 1969, visit with then-President Richard Nixon, Johnson felt "all the bombing pauses were a mistake and he had accomplished nothing" (Nixon, 1978, p. 431). Johnson reasoned that he had been misled by Soviet and Vietcong implications of a forthcoming armistice.

North, pressuring North Vietnam to stop its aggression against the South. If China reacted to our slow escalation by threatening to retaliate, we'd have plenty of time to ease off the bombing. But this control—so essential to preventing World War III—would be lost the moment we unleashed a total assault on the North.

Johnson very much feared an expansion of the war to a global dimension, as illustrated by the following comment to Kearns (1973, p. 270): "I never knew as I sat there in the afternoon, approving targets one, two, and three, whether one of those three might just be the one to set off the provisions of those secret treaties. What if one of those targets triggers off Russia or China?"

But Johnson did escalate the war, ordering more than 400,000 troops to the region by the end of 1966 and continuing the bombing campaigns. Indeed, the United States secretly expanded the geography of the war into some regions of Laos and Cambodia, citing the areas as communist troop refuges. Nuclear weapons, however, were never a key ingredient in Johnson's war policy. According to General Westmoreland (1980), the president did charge the JCS on a few occasions with analyzing the option, but never considered their use anything but improbable. This should not be surprising considering Johnson's concern with Soviet or Chinese entrance into the war; the administration believed that nuclear weapons would undoubtedly bring about World War III. Indeed, in an interview with Kearns (1973), Johnson went to great pains to explain his fight for a "conservative" bombing campaign, despite his general's desire to completely "saturate" the North Vietnamese with bombs.

In late 1968, Johnson announced he was not seeking re-election. Dejected by the failure of both the U.S. effort in Vietnam and his plans for the "Great Society," he retreated from politics for the rest of his life. Again, while there was some discussion on the issue, Johnson did not seriously consider nuclear attacks against the North Vietnamese.

Nixon and Nuclear Weapons in Vietnam

> The United States intervened in the Vietnam War to prevent North Vietnam from imposing its totalitarian government on South Vietnam through military conquest, both because a Communist victory would lead to massive human suffering for the people of Vietnam and because it would damage American strategic interests and pose a threat to our allies and friends in other non-Communist nations. (Nixon, 1985, p. 46)

> I do not believe that the United States should threaten any other nation. (Public Papers of Richard Nixon, 1971, p. 249)

Richard Nixon assumed the presidency in 1969, four years after Johnson had initiated the air attack Operation Rolling Thunder. While there are several reasons Nixon prevailed in the election, many have identified his position on the Vietnam War as a significant factor. Throughout the Vietnam War, Nixon emphasized two general goals: To win the war, and to win it "honorably." On several occasions, Nixon (1985, p. 181) made public this concern, promising he would not be "the first U.S. president to lose a war." During his tenure in the White House, he repeatedly underscored the point that the United States would not tolerate defeat, and that such a defeat would symbolize U.S. inferiority and a lack of commitment to thwarting the spread of communism.

Nixon asserted a number of times during his campaign that he had "a secret plan to end the war" and that he would "bring peace" (Haldeman, 1978; Time, 1985). The U.S. public did not know the details of this secret strategy. Nixon's plan involved the threat to use nuclear weapons, and is known as the "November Ultimatum." The scheme, known among top officials as a part of Operation Duck Hook, involved a dramatic escalation of the war and a message to the North Vietnamese that if a settlement was not reached by November 1, 1969, the United States would "be forced to take measures of the greatest consequences" (Nixon, 1978, p. 396). The plan, not dissimilar to Eisenhower's strategy some sixteen years earlier, was nuclear extortion.

Nixon had been President Eisenhower's vice-president, and possessed knowledge of the internal dynamics of the settlement of the Korean War. He firmly believed that the threat of nuclear weapons could be used against the North Vietnamese in the same way that Eisenhower had used them as a threat against the North Koreans: to scare them into an armistice. There is no question Nixon held the opinion that the chief reason for the abrupt end to the Korean War was Eisenhower's threats to use atomic weapons. At the national Republican convention in 1968, Nixon publicly announced this conviction when he stated, "I'll tell you how Korea was ended. . . . Eisenhower let the word go out diplomatically that we would not tolerate this continued ground war of attrition" (Public Papers, 1974, p. 339). In a *Time* (1985, p. 50) magazine interview, Nixon again expressed how instrumental he thought the atomic threats were in the ending of the war in Korea:

> Dulles (through Eisenhower) said "You know, we are very concerned about Korea," and the "President's patience is wearing thin," and finally saying that unless the logjam is broken, it will lead to the use of nuclear weapons. It worked. The Chinese were probably tired of the war. And the Russians did not want to go to war over Korea. But it was the Bomb that did it.

According to H. R. Haldeman (1978), one of Nixon's closest advisors, the president saw great similarity in the situation faced by Eisenhower and his predicament in the Vietnam War.

Nixon believed Eisenhower's military background distinguished him from other presidents in the sense that his threats made to foreign governments would be taken very seriously. Nixon, however, felt that his twenty-year career in promoting anticommunist policies gave him comparable leverage in times of international crisis. Haldeman (1978, p. 82) recalled his impression of Nixon during the first few weeks of his presidency:

> Nixon not only wanted to end the Vietnam War, he was absolutely convinced he would end it in his first year. I remember during the campaign, walking along a beach, he once said "I'm the one man in this country who can do it, Bob. . . . They'll believe any threat of force that Nixon makes because it's Nixon."

The president undoubtedly viewed nuclear weapons as the threat that would make "believers" out of the North Vietnamese. Haldeman (1978, p. 83) also remembered a conversation with Nixon on the secret plan, which offers the first evidence that the president strongly favored nuclear threats:

> Nixon said: "I call it the Madman Theory, Bob. I want the North Vietnamese to believe I've reached the point where I might do anything to stop the war. We'll just slip the word to them that 'for God's sake, you know Nixon is obsessed about Communism. We can't restrain him when he's angry—and he has his hand on the nuclear button'—and Ho Chi Minh himself will be in Paris in two days begging for peace."

Haldeman then identifies the messenger of the threat: "As it turned out it wasn't Bill Rogers, the future Secretary of state, who slipped the word to the North Vietnamese, but a brilliant, impulsive, witty gentleman with an engaging German accent—Henry Kissinger."

Henry Kissinger, selected as the president's assistant for

national security, engaged in secret meetings with the North Vietnamese beginning in early August 1969. These meetings were designed to ensure that the enemy was told in clear terms that the United States would no longer tolerate the present state of the war. Kissinger had been sent to Paris at least twelve times to engage in secret negotiations with the North Vietnamese. These meetings were so secret that only Nixon and a few of his advisors in the Defense and State Departments were made aware of the substance of the conversations. Nixon has offered several official reasons for this secrecy: "Privately, both sides can be more flexible in offering new approaches and also private discussions allow both sides to talk frankly, to take positions free from the pressure of public debate" (Public Papers, 1974, p. 101).

In fact, the issue of secrecy was so important that Nixon ordered his entire staff of both the State and Defense Departments to say nothing if asked "whether private talks have begun, as to when they begin, (or) as to what occurred" (Public Papers, 1971, p. 247). The Kissinger meetings in Paris exemplify this fear of exposure, and were characterized by Nixon (1978, p. 396) as "full of cloak and dagger episodes, with Kissinger riding slouched down in the back seats" of unmarked vehicles. In numerous statements it is clear that Nixon felt that if progress was to be made, it would come from these secret talks, not the public forum.

Kissinger's "nuclear diplomacy" took place on August 4, 1969. According to both Nixon's (1978) and Kissinger's (1979) memoirs, the Paris meeting was scheduled at the same time Nixon was meeting with Romanian President Nicolae Ceauşescu in Bucharest, which according to Nixon (1978, p. 394) provided "the perfect camouflage" for Kissinger's secret meeting. Nixon decided that a two-pronged approach to delivering the November ultimatum would make more of an impression on the North Vietnamese, so he informed Ceauşescu, whose government was known to have good relations with the North

Vietnamese, that "We cannot indefinitely continue to have two hundred deaths a week in Vietnam and no progress in Paris. On November 1 this year . . . if there is no progress, we must re-evaluate our policy." Nixon apparently made other remarks to the Romanian president, stressing the rationale for the deadline and indicating that the United States was prepared to take extreme measures to end the war.

The first meeting between Kissinger and North Vietnamese chief negotiators Xuan Thuy and Mai Van Bo was surprisingly blunt, with Kissinger immediately threatening to use nuclear weapons if no progress was made. As Nixon (1978, p. 396) describes, "Kissinger opened by saying that he wanted to convey a message from me personally. Kissinger said 'I have been asked to tell you in all solemnity, that if by November 1 no major progress has been made toward a solution, we will be compelled—with great reluctance—to take measures of the greatest consequence.'"

The threat produced no immediate results for the U.S. administration. While Nixon and Kissinger do not mention that the phrase "nuclear weapons" was used during this meeting, Nixon later admitted in a *Time* (1985) magazine interview that the threat had indeed been a nuclear one. The meeting ended as abruptly as it had begun, with the North Vietnamese representatives demanding complete U.S. withdrawal from the conflict. Even though the United States was threatening to unleash its weapons of mass destruction, the North Vietnamese appeared unmoved by the warning. The stalemate between the parties thus continued.

During the first stages of the series of secret discussions, Kissinger was orchestrating a special research panel to look into escalation methods. In August and September, a panel consisting of top military and political advisors examined the Navy's Duck Hook plans, which are to this day still classified, and was ordered by Kissinger to examine objectively a number of options with regard to the war and the first task will be the most difficult of all. We've had a series of talks with the North Vietnamese in Paris. We've been very forthcoming; we've attempted to make concessions which have been unrequited and I refuse to believe that a little forth-rate power like North Vietnam does not have a breaking point. . . . It shall be the assignment of this group to examine the option of a savage, decisive blow against North Vietnam. You start without any preconceptions at all. You are to sit down and map out what would be a savage blow. (Quoted in Hersch, 1983, p. 126)

Roger Morris was placed in charge of compiling the research into summary form, and had numerous private conversations with Kissinger on the panel's findings. Morris (1977) reports that at one point during the panel's discussion, someone asked Kissinger about the use of nuclear weapons. Kissinger replied somewhat in the negative, but added, "you are not to exclude the possibility of a nuclear device being used for purposes of a blockade." Morris (1977) recalls that despite Kissinger's apparent disinterest in full nuclear planning, he received several folders on target sites to be bombed by nuclear means and the predicted results of such nuclear attacks.

There are two other instances indicating that Kissinger seriously considered the nuclear weapons option. In an interview with Hersch (1983), Charles Colson, a close aide of Nixon, recalled NATO Ambassador Robert Ellsworth asserting in early 1969 that Nixon and Kissinger were planning nuclear bombings, and that the bombs would be dropped by the end of the year. Colson also added that the "word around" the Pentagon was that Kissinger had been lobbying for the use of nuclear weapons. Hersch (1983, p. 129) also discusses interviews with two scientists retained for comment on the nuclear option by both Kissinger and the special panel charged with developing a "savage, decisive blow." According to the scientists, they "knew Henry [Kissinger] was involved in the planning and that he wanted it. The implications went way beyond local tactical considerations." The scientists also reported that many were against the nuclear option because of "election politics."

In his memoirs, Nixon (1978, p. 398) remembered the dilemma he faced over the November Ultimatum:

In the weeks remaining before November 1, I wanted to orchestrate the maximum possible pressure on Hanoi. I was confident that we could bring sufficient pressure to bear on the diplomatic front. But the only chance for my ultimatum to succeed was to convince the Communists that I could depend on solid support at home if they decided to call my bluff.

Nixon (1978, p. 399) also worried over the perceived legitimacy of his threat:

having initiated a policy of pressure on North Vietnam that now involved not only our government but foreign governments as well, I felt that I had no choice but to carry it through. Faced with the prospect of demonstrations at home that I could not prevent, my only alternative was to try to make it clear to the enemy that the protests would have no effect on my decision, Otherwise my ultimatum would appear empty.

In order to make his ultimatum seem legitimate, Nixon instituted several courses of action: advanced pressure on the Soviets to engage in discussion with the North Vietnamese on an armistice; threats of terminating U.S. aid to countries that continued exporting their products to Hanoi; and leaking an exaggerated report on plans to massively invade North Vietnam as well as to institute new port blockades. The most serious episode engineered to reaffirm the ultimatum to the North Vietnamese was the movement of nuclear forces to situation DEF CON 1 in the month of October (Hersch, 1983).

The DEF CON system housed at the Pentagon is an alert device with five different levels of preparation for war, with DEF CON 1 commanding "maximum nuclear force readiness." Not since the 1962 Cuban Missile Crisis had the United States gone to this "war imminent" stage of defense. Joseph Urgo, an Air Force security sergeant, remembered being stunned by orders to guard two B-52 nuclear-equipped aircraft:

> Nobody was telling us anything. All days off were canceled and it went on and on. . . . Putting those planes on the runway freaked me out. All my experience told me that they would never take a chance by putting two nuclear-loaded airplanes out in the open. . . . Obviously we were in some sort of real situation. (Quoted in Hersch, 1983, p. 124)

In all, there were six aircraft fully loaded with tactical nuclear weapons on the military portion of the Atlantic City, New Jersey, airstrip as well as other aircraft fully loaded with nuclear bombs still hidden in the hangar. There is also evidence to suggest that dozens of nuclear-equipped airplanes around the United States were also placed on full alert. The alert lasted an unprecedented twenty-nine days, during which time nuclear forces commander Air Force Colonel Ray Sitton was told nothing about the reasons for the alert (Hersch, 1983). Undoubtedly, the reason for the DEF CON 1 stage was to make the Soviets, who were known to have been aware of the alert, pressure the North Vietnamese into ending the war, emphasizing that the U.S. nuclear threat appeared to be materializing.

It is important to note that U.S.–Soviet relations were significantly less antagonistic during the latter part of Johnson's administration and the majority of Nixon's presidency. The Soviets were still viewed with caution and suspicion, but the clashes between the superpowers which regularly occurred during the Truman, Eisenhower, and Kennedy administrations were rare in the 1960s and 1970s. But while detente between the Soviets and the United States was established, Soviet-Sino relations deteriorated.

It is well documented that Nixon and Kissinger felt the Soviets could be instrumental in influencing the North Vietnamese. Indeed, Kissinger had met with Soviet Ambassador Anatoly Dobrynin on numerous occasions in 1969 to request the Soviets' help in negotiating a settlement. Sometimes these meetings took on a strange character, as when Nixon purposely interrupted a Kissinger-Dobrynin meeting by phone to order Kissinger to say to his Soviet counterpart, "The President just told me in that call that as far as Vietnam is concerned, the train has just left the station and is now headed down the track" (Nixon, 1978, p. 399). This meeting took place just days before the full nuclear alert commenced. None of the Kissinger-Dobrynin meetings, however, resulted in any cooperation between the United States and Soviet Union on the issue. The October 1969 DEF CON 1, the readying of nuclear-equipped aircraft, and possibly the strange message from Nixon to Kissinger were clearly an attempt to buttress Nixon's ultimatum to the North Vietnamese through the Soviet Union.

Nixon was deeply frustrated with the lack of Soviet effort, and on many occasions spoke directly to Dobrynin on the issue. On October 20, at a private meeting between the two leaders, Nixon (1978, p. 407) tried to make clear to the Soviet ambassador these disappointments, while tacitly implying a reversal in detente if the Soviets did not involve themselves in ending the war:

> I want you to understand that the Soviet Union is going to
> be stuck with me for the next three years and three
> months, and during all that time I will keep in mind what

is being done right now, today. . . . All you have done is repeat the same tired old slogans that the North Vietnamese used six months ago. . . . If the Soviet Union found it possible to do something in Vietnam . . . then we might do something dramatic to improve our relations . . . but until then, I have to say any real progress will be difficult.

Again, despite such clear demands and candid scolding of the Soviets, Moscow did not involve itself, in any meaningful way, in the U.S. effort to end the war.

The plan to escalate the war on November 1 if no major progress was achieved was never enacted. While Nixon was worried about future perceptions concerning the legitimacy of threats, he notes in his memoirs that he simply could not escalate the war at that time:

> I had to decide what to do about the ultimatum. I knew that unless I had some indisputably good reason for not carrying out my threat . . . the Communists would become contemptuous of us and even more difficult to deal with. I knew, however, that after all the protests and the Moratorium, American public opinion would be seriously divided by any military escalation of the war. (Nixon, 1978, p. 402)

It is important to note two occurrences during the deliberations on the ultimatum. The war had many stages, but the 1968 Johnson bombing halt and early 1969 secret bombings of Cambodia should not be underestimated as factors associated with Nixon's nuclear strategy. While the United States was continuing the ground war, the bombing campaign had been halted by President Johnson on November 1, 1968. Nixon had not broken this moratorium because he felt that if bombings were reinstated without his administration setting a clear policy on the conflict, Johnson's work on negotiating a settlement may have been compromised. In fact, it is not unreasonable to assume that the ultimatum date, set for exactly one year after the halt of bombings, was an attempt to show the differences in strategy between the present and past administrations. Indeed, Nixon had severely criticized Johnson's handling of the war, particularly his relatively conservative approach to military bombing campaigns, arguing that a continued "ground war of attrition" without either escalation or further steps toward an armistice was an improper path. Thus, the ultimatum can be viewed not only as a threat to escalate the war, but to interject two entirely different dimensions to the conflict: the more radical position of the Nixon administration and the possibility of nuclear attacks.

The second important occurrence during the formative stages of the ultimatum was Nixon and Kissinger's secret bombings of Cambodia, a region bordering Vietnam on the west. Considerable discussion took place in March 1969 on the question of whether to bomb North Vietnam or Cambodia. Nixon (1985, p. 107) notes in his memoirs that he chose not to resume bombing the North because it would "produce a violent outburst of protest . . . [and] would have destroyed our efforts to bring the country together." Instead, the plan, known only to a handful of Nixon's advisors, was to bomb Vietcong ammunition posts in Cambodia, which were particularly damaging to the U.S. war effort. The fourteen-month, 110,000-ton bombings of Cambodia were kept under the strictest secrecy, with full public and Congressional knowledge of the events not surfacing until 1973. Both Kissinger and Nixon make clear in their memoirs the reason for the secrecy: To prevent domestic uproar.*

ANALYSIS

The factors that shaped the crime of nuclear extortion in Vietnam were very similar to those found in Korea. Nixon, like

---

*Ironically, massive U.S. public uproar ensued over U.S. actions in Cam-

Eisenhower, inherited an unpopular war in Asia that had bogged down militarily. Nixon, like Eisenhower, had pledged during his presidential campaign to end the war as quickly as possible. Nixon, in fact, had claimed to have a secret plan to end the war and this put considerable pressure on his administration to quickly accomplish the task.

In addition to the administration's goal to end the war in a timely manner, the larger structural forces that had led the United States to intervene in Korea and invade Vietnam also affected the decision (Chomsky, 1995). The Cold War battle to contain communism, the effort to defend American security interests in the Far East, and the protection of U.S. access to valued resources and markets throughout the Pacific region all required an American victory in Vietnam.

Once again, conventional military power seemed unable to provide a victory or drive the enemy to the bargaining table. A bigger stick still would perhaps do the trick, and nuclear weapons were the biggest stick available. Once again, just as in Korea, we see a kind of instrumental logic in operation that considers the use of nuclear weapons to be the most effective and efficient means to achieve the goal of victory.

The decision to actually use nuclear weapons in Vietnam was blocked by what Zinn (1995, p. 460) calls "the greatest antiwar movement the country had ever experienced." Despite his public statements at the time, Nixon later admitted in his memoirs that the antiwar movement caused him to drop his plans to intensify the war (Zinn, 1995), just as Eisenhower's concern over allied reaction forced him to forgo the actual use of atomic weapons in Korea.

Just as Eisenhower had done, Nixon turned to the threat of nuclear weapons in an effort to force a diplomatic solution to

---

bodia. Although the air attacks were kept secret, the April 1970 ground invasion of Cambodia was publicized. This led to massive student protests across the country and the infamous Ohio National Guardsmen murders of four Kent State University students.

the quagmire of Vietnam. Nixon felt that Eisenhower's use of nuclear extortion had ended the stalemate in Korea and he was convinced it could work again in Vietnam. He was wrong about that. But it wouldn't prevent other presidents from using nuclear diplomacy again in the future (Gerson, 1995).

5

Nuclear Weapons Production and the Contamination of the Environment

Since World War II, the U.S. government has become increasingly dependent on weapons of mass destruction as an instrument of foreign policy. As a result, it constructed a large and sprawling production complex to manufacture and assemble nuclear weapons. The production of nuclear weapons, unfortunately, has led to massive pollution of the environment (Makhijani, Hu, and Yih, 1995). Radioactive and other hazardous wastes have contaminated the air, soil, and water at most of the nuclear weapons production facilities around the country, often in violation of federal environmental law.

THE HISTORY OF ATOMIC AND NUCLEAR WEAPONS PRODUCTION

The United States' production of atomic energy began in 1942 when a team of scientists led by Enrico Fermi succeeded in achieving the first controlled, self-sustained nuclear reaction.

This chapter is in part based on an article by Kauzlarich and Kramer that originally appeared in *Journal of Human Justice* 5 (1): 4–28. Used with permission.

Within months, the Manhattan Engineering District was formed with the sole mission of developing atomic weapons. In 1942, under the military supervision of General Leslie Groves and the scientific supervision of J. Robert Oppenheimer, three facilities were created to develop the atomic bomb. Los Alamos, New Mexico, was chosen to be the site for the design, testing, and assembly of atomic weapons. In Hanford, Washington, a facility was created to produce plutonium, and in Oak Ridge, Tennessee, a uranium-separation plant was created. These three facilities combined to form the $2 billion enterprise called the Manhattan Project.

These facilities operated in extreme secrecy both outside and inside the complex (Center for Defense Information, 1989; Clarfield and Wiecek, 1984; Cochran, 1988; Powaski, 1987; Williams and Cantelon, 1984). As Weiner (1990, p. 20) states, secrecy "had become as crucial a component of the bomb as uranium." Clarfield and Wiecek (1984, p. 34) describe the secrecy at one of the earliest facilities:

> The residents of Los Alamos became, in some sense, nonpersons. Children born there could not have the location entered on their birth certificates. No one was allowed to tell the families and friends they left behind where they lived. Army counter-intelligence corps personnel read all outgoing as well as incoming mail. All buildings except housing and community facilities were restricted-access, enforced by security badges.

The activities of the Manhattan Project were hidden very well. Until 1944, "funds for the project came either from the military departments, which concealed their purpose, or from a special contingency fund appropriated for the President which was shielded from congressional scrutiny" (Powaski, 1987, p. 7). The activities of the complex were so secret, in fact, that when Harry Truman assumed the presidency in 1945, he had absolutely no knowledge of the Manhattan Project (Clarfield and Wiecek, 1984; Powaski, 1987; Williams and Cantelon, 1984).

The primary reason for the extreme secrecy surrounding the activities of the Manhattan Project was that the United States feared German access to the bomb (Powaski, 1987; Williams and Cantelon, 1984). The Roosevelt administration feared the leakage of information so much that, in addition to keeping the activities of the project secret from the Germans, it also kept the information away from the U.S. Congress, media, and public (Clarfield and Wiecek, 1984; Powaski, 1987). The Germans had entered World War II with the lead in nuclear research: Otto Hohn and Fritz Strassman had already split the atom in 1938; the Third Reich controlled one of the richest sources of uranium in the world; and Germany had been pursuing the development of atomic weapons at least four years longer than the United States (Powaski, 1987).

The Manhattan scientists were made very much aware of the German threat, and were pressured to "beat Germany to the bomb" (Powaski, 1987; Williams and Cantelon, 1984). This was not, however, the only motivation for the hurried development of the bomb. After the German surrender, Oppenheimer stated, "I don't think there was any time we worked harder at the speed-up than in the period after the German surrender" (quoted in Powaski, 1987, p. 12). There were two reasons for this: the Japanese threat, and the Soviet threat.

After the German surrender, the only immediate threat to the United States was Japan. As early as 1944, Roosevelt and Churchill agreed that when a bomb "is finally available, it might, perhaps, after mature consideration, be used against the Japanese" (quoted in Powaski, 1987, p. 13). On August 6, 1945, only months after Truman took office, and days after the first usable forms of plutonium and uranium were produced at Hanford and Oak Ridge, the United States dropped a uranium bomb on Hiroshima. Three days later, on August 9, a plutonium bomb was dropped on Nagasaki. Both Japanese cities were destroyed. A Navy officer (quoted in Rhodes, 1986, p. 742) described the aftereffects: "A smell of death and corruption pervades the place. The general impression, which transcends those derived from the evidence of our physical senses, is one of deadness, the absolute essence of death in the sense of finality without hope of resurrection. It's everywhere, and nothing has escaped its touch." In total, nearly 400,000 people died as a result of the bombings (Rhodes, 1986). The United States had clearly shown the world that it had the ability to harness nuclear energy. After this awesome display of power, the Japanese surrendered.

The United States' concern over losing its monopoly on nuclear power to the Soviets surfaced prior to the dropping of the atomic bombs on Japan. In April 1945, the United States ordered its army to bomb the nuclear production facilities in Berlin. The Germans were making significant progress toward the creation of atomic weapons. The purpose of this mission was to destroy laboratories and other facilities that were associated with nuclear energy before the planned Soviet invasion of Berlin, scheduled a few months later (Powaski, 1987). The reason for the mission, code named Alsos, was clear. As General Groves stated, "our principal concern was to keep information and atomic secrets from falling into the hands of Russia" (quoted in Powaski, 1987, p. 40). In the end, the operation succeeded, and Russia was denied access to the blueprints for the new weapon.

The end of World War II signified the beginning of a massive effort on the part of the United States to increase the sophistication of atomic weapons. At this time, the U.S. military, the primary beneficiary of nuclear energy research, lost control of the rights to produce atomic weapons. Considerable debate took place between the proponents of placing atomic energy under civilian control, principally advocated by the Federation of Atomic Scientists, and those who wanted atomic energy to stay in the hands of the military. In the end, the scientists won the legislative battle. The Atomic Energy Act of 1946, sometimes referred to as the McMahon bill, established the independent civilian-controlled Atomic Energy Commission (AEC). Under this act, the military could only gain access to the bomb by a direct presidential order. Although the AEC, in principle, was a civilian body, the military had an enormous influence over atomic energy policies and operations (Clarfield and Wiecek, 1984; Powaski, 1987). As Powaski (1987, p. 123) explains:

> Organizationally, military emphasis was built into the structure of the AEC from the beginning. One of its four operating divisions was military applications. A military liaison committee was appointed by the Department of Defense to participate in the AEC's weapons work. The armed services retained for themselves the intelligence function of the Manhattan Project, rather than transferring it to the AEC. The ties were so close that an incoming secretary of defense is supposed to have asked, after being shown the Department of Defense organization chart "Where is the AEC?"

One of the first postwar responsibilities of the AEC was the transformation of military applications of nuclear energy to civilian uses (Powaski, 1987). Robert Oppenheimer, the chair of the AEC, clearly wanted to see a complete effort toward this goal, and argued vehemently for the peaceful application of atomic energy (Powaski, 1987). Enrico Fermi, the scientist credited with the first successful attempt at generating a sustained nuclear reaction, and who also resided high in the AEC hierarchy, argued that primacy should be directed toward future weapons programs. In the end, according to Powaski (1987, p. 111), "The Fermi view prevailed, and the recommendation for priority in weapons was instrumental in committing the AEC to the same view, which in turn was the basis for

President Truman's policy decision to make weapons the highest priority of the American atomic energy program."

The AEC never was required to monitor the environmental effects of the production of nuclear materials. The AEC also neglected to consider and create policy that would control the adverse environmental effects occurring during the production of nuclear weapons and nuclear materials (Steele, 1989). As former AEC General Manager Carroll L. Wilson stated in 1979, "Nobody got brownie points for caring about nuclear waste. The Atomic Energy Commission neglected the problem" (Steele, 1989, p. 19).

From 1945 to 1953, Truman embarked on a massive buildup of nuclear weapons by creating nine new production facilities. A major reason cited for this buildup was the threat of the Soviet Union. The Soviets, in 1949, successfully tested an atomic bomb, ending the U.S. monopoly and "inaugurating the era of proliferation" (Williams and Cantelon, 1984, p. 114). From this time on, relations between the United States and the Soviet Union dictated, to a large degree, the quantity and quality of the U.S. production of nuclear weapons.

Soon after the Soviets tested their first atomic bomb, a meeting was called between Truman and the AEC's chair David Lilienthal. Lilienthal was planning on presenting a report to Truman that argued against the development of the newly conceptualized hydrogen bomb. Truman did not read the report and, after confirming that the Soviets could build such a weapon, ordered the development of the hydrogen bomb. Recalling the meeting later, Lilienthal wrote that his effort to block the development of the hydrogen bomb was like saying "no to a steam roller" (Powaski, 1987, p. 57). The AEC, he felt, had become nothing more than a major contractor to the Department of Defense (Powaski, 1987).

The decision to develop the hydrogen bomb was also conducted in extreme secrecy (Clarfield and Wiecek, 1984; Powaski, 1987; Williams and Cantelon, 1984). Similar to the secrecy surrounding the initial development of the bomb during the Manhattan era, "there was no public, or even congressional debate, over the decision to develop the hydrogen bomb" (Powaski, 1987, p. 57). Thus, similar circumstances surrounded the two major decisions to develop atomic weapons: both were conducted in secrecy; both projects operated under no formal or informal social control; and both decisions were based on the threat of an outside nation or nations. This prompted immense pressure on atomic scientists and the AEC to perform a sole function—developing bombs.

On the same day that Truman approved the production of the hydrogen bomb, he also operationalized the suggestions called for in a report called NSC-68, discussed earlier. This study called "for an enormous increase in American defense spending in order to prevent Soviet domination of the world" (Powaski, 1987, p. 217). Thus, the nine new nuclear weapons production facilities were created to accommodate this mission.

The Atomic Energy Act of 1946 was replaced by the Atomic Energy Act of 1954. Most of the specific provisions of the new act, however, and all the licensing and related regulatory requirements applied solely to commercial reactors. Thus, the Act of 1954 did little to change the prior act in relation to the government's use of nuclear energy (Clarfield and Wiecek, 1984). The government's nuclear weapons production complex remained exempt from any real outside monitoring and did not have to follow the somewhat strict regulations on the emerging civilian nuclear industry. Despite Eisenhower's "Atoms for Peace" plan, the military application of nuclear energy grew substantially during these years.

The production of nuclear weapons peaked between the late 1950s and early 1960s. During this time, twenty military nuclear weapons facilities were operating at peak capacity (Cochran, 1988). As Weiner (1990, p. 35) describes, "By 1958, nuclear weaponry was an infinitely expanding dynamo. The target list had grown to some 20,000 dots on the communist map. The target list included every city in Russia, Eastern Europe, and China." By 1960, "Three thousand two hundred and sixty-seven nuclear warheads [could] annihilate the Soviet Union, China and Eastern Europe in a single blinding blow. They planned to follow this apocalyptic spasm with thousands, and thousands of more bombs. Ten nations would be obliterated. Five hundred million people would die."

During the Kennedy years (1961–63), nuclear weapons production reached its zenith, with over 5,000 weapons produced each year (Cochran, 1988). Along with the tense climate of the Cold War and the residual effects of McCarthyism, the antagonistic relations between the Soviet Union and the United States accelerated with events such as the Berlin Crisis and the Cuban Missile Crisis (see Powaski, 1987). Between 1964 and 1976, however, nuclear weapons production decreased. President Johnson shut down ten weapons-production facilities because of abundant stocks of plutonium (Cochran, 1988). The SALT talks, and the attitude of some high level officials in the government (particularly Johnson's Secretary of Defense Robert S. McNamara) that weapons proliferation was futile, fostered this cutback in nuclear weapons production (Powaski, 1987; Williams and Cantelon, 1984).

THE ORGANIZATION OF THE DEPARTMENT OF ENERGY'S PRODUCTION COMPLEX

In 1974, the Energy Reorganization Act abolished the Atomic Energy Commission and established two new organizations: the Energy Research and Development Administration (ERDA), and the Nuclear Regulatory Commission (NRC). This legislation was enacted in response to concerns that the AEC was functioning as both regulator (of civilian industries), and promoter of nuclear programs (through the military) (Powaski, 1987; Radioactive Waste Campaign, 1988). ERDA was established to oversee the promotional and defense productions, while the regulating and licensing operations for commercial nuclear power were assigned to the NRC (Radioactive Waste Campaign, 1988).

The Department of Energy (DOE) was formed by President Carter to "give a clear direction and focus to America's energy future by providing the framework for carrying out a comprehensive, balanced energy policy" (U.S. Department of Energy, 1979, p. 2). As a part of orchestrating this "new direction," the Department of Energy was given the responsibility of producing nuclear weapons. Although manufacturing nuclear weapons is only a fraction of DOE's responsibilities, it has traditionally devoted one-third of its funds to warhead production (Lamperti, 1984a).

The basic mission of DOE defense activities during the Cold War was to produce material for nuclear weapons and to manufacture fuel for the U.S. Navy (U.S. General Accounting Office, 1986). The DOE oversaw the production of nuclear weapons and materials at seventeen major facilities around the country: six facilities produced nuclear material only, six plants produced nuclear material and assembled components into warheads, and five facilities designed and tested nuclear weapons. Almost all of these facilities were created in the 1940s and 1950s.

The entire complex employed over 100,000 workers and has consistently had annual budgets of approximately 8 billion dollars (Center for Defense Information, 1989). The DOE, like its predecessors the AEC and ERDA, carried out most of its programs by contracting with private firms and universities. Most of the contractors who operated the majority of the DOE facilities were large, multinational corporations such as Westinghouse, DuPont, General Electric, and Martin Marietta.

The U.S. government owned the equipment and materials used in the manufacturing of nuclear weapons items, and directed the contractor to produce the final product, that is, the warheads themselves or the converted nuclear materials. Thus, the contractor was responsible for the actual production of the nuclear weapons, while the DOE acted as a supervisor of the contractor's activities. The organization of the entire weapons complex has much in common with the system that developed during the Manhattan Project era (Cochran, 1988; Lamperti, 1984b; Powaski, 1987) in which private contractors maintain the important roles of researcher, developer, and manufacturer of the entire nuclear weapons program.

The DOE-Contractor Relationship

There were two kinds of financial arrangements the DOE made with its contractors. Some contractors operated on a nonprofit basis, for which they received compensation only for the costs incurred during the production of nuclear weapons. Other contractors operated on a profit basis, or "award fee" arrangement. In this type of contract, DOE agreed to pay a contractor bonus money if, during a six-month period, the contractor met certain preestablished criteria. Although each contract the DOE made with its corporate operators was different, most contracts contained essentially the same provisions (Alverez, 1990; Mobilization for Survival, 1989).

The DuPont corporation operated the Savannah River Plant in Aiken, South Carolina, from the inception of the atomic age. On a nonprofit basis, DuPont had been held responsible for the day-to-day operations of the facility. One clause in the DOE-DuPont (National Academy of Sciences, 1987, p. 44) contract read:

> The Contractor shall take all reasonable precautions in the performance of the work under this Contract to protect the safety of employees and of members of the public and to minimize dangers from all hazards to life and property, and shall comply with all health, safety, and fire protection regulations and requirements.

The same provision was included in DOE's 1987 contract with UNC Nuclear Industries, the operator of the Hanford facility located in Hanford, Washington. The only difference between the two contracts, in relation to the mandates of the DOE concerning the contractor's obligation to perform all activities in compliance with applicable environmental laws, was that UNC operated under a profit arrangement with the DOE, whereas DuPont operated its facility under a nonprofit arrangement (National Academy of Sciences, 1987). In all other matters, the DOE placed the bulk of the responsibility on the contractor to operate the facilities in a lawful manner.

The National Academy of Sciences (1987) has argued that DOE directives to their contractors were often vague and that they provided the corporations with a great deal of latitude in the interpretation of DOE orders. For example, in the 1987 DOE-UNC contract, the DOE ordered UNC to "operate and monitor the N Reactor and support facilities in a safe, secure, and environmentally sound manner to achieve a fiscal year production goal of 705 KMWD, with less than 24 unscheduled outage days" (National Academy of Sciences, 1987, p. 51). While this directive may be legally inclusive, the DOE does not provide the contractor with the specific methods to achieve compliance with applicable environmental issues; in this sense, the DOE orders could be considered relatively vague. Additionally, the above clause seems to indicate that the DOE sent a message to the contractor that while safe and environmentally sound procedures of waste disposal (which are unspecified) are important, it was equally important that precise production quotas be met.

The Organizational Management Structure

The complex used a three-tier approach to carry out its operations. The first tier was the contractor who actually performed the day-to-day operations. The contractor developed its own environmental protection program and periodically checked on its implementation through internal audits and self-appraisals (U.S. General Accounting Office, 1986). The contractor was held responsible to meet all DOE environmental, health, and safety requirements as a condition of the contract between the DOE and the contractor (Walker, 1986). Thus, the contractor had a high degree of responsibility in ensuring that the work was carried out in compliance with all applicable environmental laws (Alverez, 1990; National Academy of Sciences, 1987; U.S. General Accounting Office, 1986).

The second tier of the management structure resided in the DOE itself. The DOE field offices were directly responsible for overseeing the contractors' performance. The field offices periodically conducted appraisals and audits on the contractors' work including incident releases and quality assurance (U.S. General Accounting Office, 1986).

The final tier of the management structure was the general oversight by DOE headquarters. The office of the Assistant Secretary for Environment, Safety and Health held primary responsibility for the entire complex's compliance with environmental law. There were three ways this was done: (1) appraising the field offices' environmental protection activities, (2) reviewing plans for each field office on how it was going to carry out its respective environmental programs, and (3) reviewing accidents and unusual occurrences at DOE facilities (U.S. General Accounting Office, 1986).

THE CRIMINAL CONTAMINATION OF THE ENVIRONMENT

Producing nuclear weapons resulted in a large amount of radioactive and nonradioactive (hazardous) waste (Lamperti, 1984b; Office of Technology Assessment, 1991; Reicher and Scher, 1988; U.S. Department of Energy, 1995c; U.S. General Accounting Office, 1985, 1986, 1989). In 1986, the Savannah facility generated over 200,000 gallons of waste each day, and the Hanford plant has dumped over 200 billion gallons of radioactive and hazardous wastes since its inception in 1942 (Steele, 1989). Indeed, the contamination wrought by nuclear weapons production is so severe that estimates of forcing the complex into compliance with applicable environmental laws are a startling $400 billion (Congressional Budget Office, 1994).

The waste disposal practices employed by most of the DOE facilities historically were grounded in the theory that "soil absorbs radioactive and hazardous elements in waste, and harmlessly extinguishes all potentially dangerous chemicals" (U.S. General Accounting Office, 1986, p. 31). Thus, seepage basins and waste ponds were used as containers to filter out the harmful elements in the waste. The problem with this method of disposal, employed since the beginning of the atomic age, was that soil does not, in fact, prevent harmful elements in waste from seeping into groundwater basins (U.S. General Accounting Office, 1986). A dramatic example of this is found in the waste disposal practices of the Savannah River facility. Because of their methods of waste disposal, the Tuscaloosa Aquifer, part of the Tuscaloosa Group Formation of underground water passages, is now contaminated with several harmful elements including tritium and nitrates (U.S. General Accounting Office, 1986).*

The Hanford facility and the Savannah River Plant have been identified by several commentators as being two of the most environmentally damaging nuclear weapons facilities (Mobilization for Survival, 1989; Saleska and Makhijani, 1990; Steele, 1989; U.S. Department of Energy, 1995c). Both facilities were involved in the production of plutonium and tritium, compounds that play an integral role in making completed

---

*Tritium is a radioactive isotope that is very hazardous when assimilated into the body. Excessive nitrate levels in drinking water have been found to be harmful to all animals, especially human infants (U.S. Department of Energy, 1995d).

warheads. The Mobilization for Survival (1989, p. 3) has documented the existence of several adverse environmental consequences wrought by the activities of the Hanford facility:

> 100 square miles of groundwater are contaminated with radioactive tritium, iodine, and toxic chemicals. Over a half million gallons of high level radioactive waste [have] leaked from underground tanks and more continues to leak into the soil. Billions of gallons of liquid wastes and waste water with chemical and radioactive elements have been dumped in Hanford soil, contaminating the Columbia River and its watershed.

Steele (1989) has also documented the history of the horrible disregard for the environment that has taken place at Hanford since the beginning of the atomic age: between 1944 and 1955, 537,000 curies of unfiltered airborne releases of iodine were let loose into the atmosphere; between 1952 and 1967, ruthenium-contaminated nitrate flakes fell on nearby farmers' fields, and ultimately resulted in the death of several hundred cattle; and over sixty "lost" burial sites of waste have not been found because of the secret methods of waste disposal used by World War II scientists. The Hanford facility, which is responsible for incredibly high levels of tritium in drinking water as well as leaks from barrels containing high-level radioactive waste, has a long record of abuse and neglect concerning the environment (Office of Technology Assessment, 1991; U.S. Department of Energy, 1995d). Indeed, the Congressional Budget Office (1994) has determined that the cost of cleaning up this facility will be nearly $1.5 billion.

Equally poor is the Savannah River Plant's environmental record, which according to the Congressional Budget Office (1994) will need at least $757 million for cleanup. The groundwater near the plant is contaminated with nearly all forms of radioactive and hazardous waste, and over 51 million gallons of highly dangerous toxins are stored in leaking underground tanks beneath the facility (Mobilization for Survival, 1989). Other problems include massive mercury leaks into the air, and high levels of tritium, strontium, and iodine in the soil (Office of Technology Assessment, 1991).

The DOE regulated itself for radioactive releases into ground and surface water, radioactive waste, and radioactive leaks into water. The three principal environmental laws relevant to the DOE are the Clean Water Act of 1972, the Clean Air Act of 1970, and the Resource Conservation and Recovery Act (RCRA) of 1976. The DOE fought the applicability of these laws to their operations for several years. Especially tenacious was the DOE's refusal to comply with RCRA. In the eight years between the 1976 passage of RCRA and the 1984 district court ruling that the DOE was subject to this law, the DOE argued that under the Atomic Energy Act of 1954, their activities were exempt from the law because of "national security" (Radioactive Waste Campaign, 1988; Reicher and Scher, 1988).

RCRA gives the Environmental Protection Agency (EPA) the authority to regulate DOE's hazardous waste disposal practices. DOE's activities generate an enormous amount of hazardous waste, and it is commonly said that they are out of compliance with this law (Alverez, 1990; Center for Defense Information, 1988; Cochran, 1988; Radioactive Waste Campaign, 1988; Reicher and Scher, 1988; U.S. General Accounting Office, 1985, 1986, 1989). Millions of gallons of hazardous waste surround some DOE facilities, and all of the production sites have been found to be operating in violation of RCRA (Radioactive Waste Campaign, 1988; U.S. Department of Energy, 1995d; U.S. General Accounting Office, 1986). In a 1986 study conducted by the U.S. General Accounting Office (1986), all seven of the facilities reviewed were radically out of compliance with RCRA. Under RCRA (1976) an operator must identify its hazardous wastes; receive a permit in order to treat, store, or dispose of such wastes; monitor ground water at waste sites; close and care for sites that are taken out of operation;

and undertake corrective action. In 1985, a report by the Ohio EPA also found numerous violations of RCRA at the Fernald Feeds Materials Plant, Fernald, Ohio. It must be understood that historically, safe waste-disposal practices were largely ignored because there were no laws applicable to the production complex. Indeed, extreme amounts of hazardous wastes were disposed of at most DOE facilities, including the Y-12 plant in Oak Ridge, Tennessee, where four waste disposal plants were found to be leaking 4.7 million gallons of metal, acids, and solvents between the years of 1953 and 1963 (Reicher and Scher, 1988).

The most publicized violations of environmental laws by the DOE and a DOE contractor are found in the June 1988 Federal Bureau of Investigation (FBI) and EPA raid on the Rocky Flats facility near Denver. Rocky Flats manufactured the plutonium parts of nuclear warhead cores and various other fission bomb components (Abas, 1989). The FBI raid was prompted by Jim Stone, a six-year Rocky Flats engineer, who uncovered an internal DOE memo describing the operations at Rocky Flats as "patently illegal" and "in poor condition generally in terms of environmental compliance" (Abas, 1989, p. 22). Stone contacted the FBI, and search warrants were issued to search the facility for possible violations of environmental law. The seventy-five-member team that raided the facility was looking for evidence to substantiate the allegations that Rocky Flats had (a) illegally treated, stored, and disposed of hazardous waste in violation of RCRA; (b) discharged pollutants without a permit in violation of RCRA and the Clean Water Act; and (c) concealed environmental contamination (Abas, 1989; U.S. House, 1993).

The raid on Rocky Flats marked the first time a governmental agency had gathered evidence against another federal facility for the purposes of criminal prosecution. The operation resulted in the filing of criminal charges against the Rockwell corporation, the contractor for Rocky Flats. Rockwell responded by suing the DOE, alleging that their company was forced to violate hazardous-waste laws because the government had failed to provide a permanent storage site for liquid wastes contaminated with nonradioactive toxins (Abas, 1989). In the end, however, Rockwell dropped its lawsuit against the DOE and pleaded guilty to several violations of RCRA, the Clean Water Act, and the Clean Air Act. The plea bargain reached between the Department of Justice and Rockwell cost the company over $18.5 million (Haynes, 1997; U.S. House, 1993).

There is no question that most, if not all, of the DOE's nuclear weapons production facilities have engaged in illegal activity. With the exception of the 1989 Rocky Flats raid and subsequent prosecution, however, official EPA and U.S. Department of Justice policy is not to take criminal action against another federal agency over environmental compliance problems (Porter, 1986, p. 9; U.S. Congress, 1993). Other problems exist concerning the enforcement of environmental crimes committed by the DOE. As the Center for Defense Information (1989, p. 2) stated, "The EPA is further handicapped by overlapping laws, a lack of statistical data on military environmental compliance, military reluctance to accept EPA oversight, and the fact that government agencies are constitutionally barred from suing each other to force compliance with the law."

Although the EPA is precluded by Article 3 of the U.S. Constitution from prosecuting another federal entity, it is not precluded from investigating alleged criminal violations by individuals at federal facilities (Thompson, 1989). The contractors, however, look at the problem of enforcement in a different manner. George B. Merrick (1987, p. 6), former vice president of the Rockwell corporation, offers this grievance concerning DOE and EPA enforcement policy at the Rocky Flats facility,

We are in a position where the Department of Energy requires us to continue to produce weapons under threat of civil penalties even though the EPA and Justice Department threaten to prosecute our people and our company for operations essential to that production. We think that such governmental conduct is unfair, illegal, and unconstitutional.

ANALYSIS

The end of the Cold War and the revelation of massive radioactive contamination at DOE sites around the country have combined to nearly shut down the nuclear weapons production complex. Most of the facilities are closed and awaiting decontamination and general cleanup. The future of the complex is not clear. What is clear is that most, if not all, of the nuclear weapons production facilities in the United States have illegally contaminated the environment for over fifty years.

Goal Formation

There is little question that organizations carry out most of their activities in order to reach operative goals. Most organizational theorists stress the importance of understanding an organization's goals if one seeks insight into organizational behavior. Let us briefly consider the nuclear weapons production complex's goals, and the manner in which they were shaped by structural and historical exigencies.

As we have discussed, the United States has been engaged in or preparing for war for nearly sixty years. Given that the Cold War military strategies were largely organized around the capabilities of nuclear weapons, and that use of atomic weapons played a significant role in ending the hostilities of World War II, the production of nuclear weapons became one of the most important programs of the U.S. government. This meant that the organization charged with the responsibility of developing and producing nuclear weapons warheads had to be, among other things, highly goal oriented and concerned with performance. Indeed, the United States depended on these powerful weapons to deter Soviet aggression, and to gain economic and geopolitical advantages over those countries which did not possess nuclear weapons.

Throughout the Cold War, geopolitical and economic interests caused the United States to continually upgrade its stockpile of weapons of mass destruction, which in turn forced the nuclear weapons production complex to be even more concerned with the achievement of production goals. The United States had to match or beat every Soviet advance in nuclear technology. For example, after the Soviets' first test of a nuclear weapon, Truman gave orders to strengthen existing nuclear weapons production programs and to start production on the hydrogen bomb. Historical evidence, then, supports the contention that the weapons complex's strong commitment to producing nuclear weapons is a result of the U.S. interest in exercising global economic and political domination (Chomsky, 1988; Ellsburg, 1981; Zinn, 1995).

The Selection of Means

The methods employed to produce nuclear weapons have resulted in tremendous contamination of the environment. It is highly unlikely that the Manhattan scientists were unaware of the adverse consequences of nuclear weapons production, given their relatively sophisticated understanding of the destructive capabilities of nuclear weapons. Moreover, former AEC General Manager Wilson admitted that the AEC neglected the problem of contamination occurring as a result of weapons production. There is little question that the production goals of the weapons complex historically have taken primacy, while the adverse environmental consequences of weapons production have never been a major concern of the contractors, the DOE, or its predecessors. Several commentators, including the

DOE (1995) have agreed with this conclusion (Alverez, 1990; Center for Defense Information, 1989; Hodges, 1991; Krater, 1991; Mobilization for Survival, 1989; National Academy of Sciences, 1987; Reicher and Scher, 1988; U.S. House, 1993).

The Manhattan Project was given one objective: To produce the atomic bomb. At that time, there was little knowledge about the program by anyone who was not directly involved in it. Because the operation was conducted in such secrecy and without oversight, the weapons complex was free to use any means available to meet its objectives. Thus, the scientists and the military officials in charge of the project had great autonomy and could simply select the most effective means possible for achieving their goals. Because there was complete state sponsorship of the endeavor, any method that facilitated goal attainment could be adopted as policy.

Oversight

Many students of the nuclear weapons production complex have identified the lack of interorganizational oversight within the complex as a contributor to the resulting environmental problems (Alverez, 1990; Mobilization for Survival, 1989; National Academy of Sciences, 1987). In the most comprehensive study, conducted by the National Academy of Sciences (1987), several specific problems were cited:

1. DOE's overreliance on the contractors to conduct their activities in compliance with environmental laws

2. Weak ties between the DOE's Environmental, Safety and Health Department and the field offices

3. The need for strengthening the capability of the field offices to monitor contractor activities

4. Episodic and narrowly focused audits and appraisals into the safety of production reactors

5. DOE's lack of offices and divisions charged with research, reactor regulation, inspections, and event analysis (as compared with the NRC).

Given the insights of the National Academy, it is possible to identify three general problems in the management structure that contribute to the lack of interorganizational oversight within the complex: A lack of communication between the various parties involved in the production of nuclear weapons and materials; DOE's apparent lack of concern for appraising the operations of the contractors; and an overreliance on the contractors to conduct their operations in compliance with applicable laws.

These three problems with the interorganizational oversight of the complex have surfaced simultaneously at some points. For example, in the years between 1981 and 1987, comprehensive DOE headquarters appraisals of contractor performance occurred only twice at the Savannah facility, and only once at the Hanford plant (National Academy of Sciences, 1987).

The lack of interorganizational oversight within the weapons complex seems to be the result of the lack of concern, conveyed by both the DOE and its contractors, with the adverse environmental consequences of weapons production. Many of these problems seem to reflect the general ideology of the complex, that is, the apparent disregard for the environmental consequences of warhead production and a sole emphasis on production goals.

Organizational Culture

Because the weapons production complex of the early 1990s had many similarities to that of the earlier weapons operations, it is reasonable to speculate that an organizational "culture" or "philosophy" has developed within the complex. For example, U.S. Secretary of Energy Watkins (quoted in Olshansky and Williams, 1988, p. 29) has stated that the DOE possesses

> an underlying philosophy that adequate production of defense materials and a healthy, safe environment were not compatible objectives. A culture of mismanagement and ineptitude will have to be overcome in [this] department before the nation's troubled nuclear weapons manufacturing plants can be brought into compliance with environmental laws.

This statement supports the notions that environmental criminality has existed for some time and that production goals have historically taken precedence over concerns about the environmental consequences of warhead production; it is an integral part of the weapons complex's culture. Senator John Glenn (quoted in Steele, 1989, p. 17) makes a similar claim:

> The Department of Energy and its predecessors have been carrying out their mission to produce nuclear weapons with an attitude of neglect bordering on contempt for environmental protection. What they've said [the DOE] in effect is "we're going to build bombs and the environment be damned."

Because of the peculiar history of the weapons complex (as a governmental endeavor that supplied the nation's most important military weapons), the complex operated for a sustained period of time without being subject to external, independent review. This feature of the complex may have permitted the formation of an organizational culture that was autonomous and virtually immune to outside criticism.

Of the many characteristics of the organization of the weapons production complex, perhaps the most apparent is its tradition of the normalization of deviance. As a result of placing primacy on production goals through the most expedient and effective means, the complex has engaged in, and continues to engage in, the illegal disposal and storage of nuclear waste. These illegal practices, then, can be seen as a logical result of the organization's patterned method of operation. Since virtually every weapons production facility is or has operated in violation of one or more environmental laws, the organization as a whole could be viewed as a "culture" of noncompliance.

6

Human Radiation Experiments

The medical trials at Nuremberg in 1947 deeply impressed upon the world that experimentation with unknowing human subjects is morally and legally unacceptable.
— Justice William Brennan, 1987,
United States v. *Stanley*

The Nuremberg Code outlaws nonconsensual, reckless, and coercive experiments, and also requires that subjects be fully informed of the purposes and risks associated with the study in which they are participating. Our goal in this chapter is to describe various U.S. governmental agencies' violations of the Code through their involvement in human radiation experiments.

There have been literally thousands of human radiation experiments conducted under official U.S. auspices since the end of World War II (U.S. Department of Energy, 1995a).* The le-

---

*Until recently there has been a scarcity of public information on any state-sponsored human experimental programs. However, this has changed dramatically with the end of the Cold War and the Clinton administration's order for the declassification of hundreds of state documents. Though revelations about questionable experiments have occasionally surfaced (e.g., the 1960s CIA drug tests), nothing compares to the recent explosion of public information about the government's human

gality and morality of such experiments have been questioned by the popular press, governmental watchdog groups, and even some members of the U.S. Congress. Since there are so many cases of reckless governmental experimentation, we cannot explore all of the actors and agencies involved in these experiments. We will, however, provide a general overview of the history of U.S. human radiation experimentation, and then focus on two experiments: The 1945–47 plutonium injection experiments, and the 1962–72 testicular radiation of Washington and Oregon state prisoners.

HISTORICAL OVERVIEW OF U.S. HUMAN RADIATION EXPERIMENTS

It is desired that no document be released which refers to experiments with humans and might have [sic] adverse effect on public opinion or result in legal suit. Documents covering such work field should be classified "secret." (AEC member Haywood, 1947, p. 1)

Beginning with the 1942 Manhattan Project, scientists involved in atomic energy production realized that there was a need to understand the effects of radiation on the human body. Animal experimentation allowed for some degree of inference, but these tests revealed that different animals react to elements such as plutonium and uranium in very different ways.

---

radiation experiments. In January 1994, President Clinton ordered the creation of the Advisory Committee on Human Radiation Experiments, a group mandated to investigate all facets of the U.S. government's involvement in human-subject studies. This group used its authority to collect millions of pages of documents from at least a dozen state agencies that at one time or another supported studies using human subjects. Many of the formerly secret and classified memos are now available to the public. The Department of Energy has established an electronic database (DOE HREX) which includes hundreds of scanned documents, many of them recently declassified, relating to human radiation experimentation.

Soon, a complicated but very disjointed human experimentation program was established. The Manhattan Project and its successors were primarily responsible for providing the funds, samples, and resources to both private researchers and state-employed scholars for human radiation research.* The Manhattan Project and the Atomic Energy Commission worked with hundreds of agencies, institutions, and researchers; hospitals in Oak Ridge, Tennessee, and Elgin, Illinois, were involved as well as the hospitals at the University of Chicago, Northwestern University, and the University of Rochester. U.S.–owned and –operated nuclear weapons production and labs sites such as Argonne National Laboratory, Brookhaven National Laboratory, the Hanford plant, Lawrence Livermore Laboratory, and Los Alamos National Laboratory carried out much research on radiation as well (U.S. Department of Energy, 1995a). The Manhattan Project and its successors were faced with the enormous task of keeping track of the complex and somewhat convoluted network of human radiation experiment sites.

Examples of Human Radiation Experiments

In general, the goals of nearly all the human radiation experiments were to discern (a) the medicinal values of radiation on persons with diseases such as cancer or diabetes, (b) the health effects of radiation on nuclear weapons production workers, and (c) the human body's reaction to radiation from atomic and nuclear weapons explosions (Advisory Committee on Human Radiation Experiments, 1995). These goals, noble as they were, were pursued by the state and by researchers without any real kind of social control or organizational supervision (U.S. Department of Energy, 1995a); this lack of such oversight

---

*The Manhattan Project was succeeded by the Atomic Energy Commission in 1947, then in 1974 the organization was renamed the Energy Research and Development Administration. Finally, in 1977, nuclear weapons–related activities were housed within the Department of Energy.

was one of a number of factors contributing to the criminal manner in which many of the experiments were conducted. Indeed, even the U.S. Department of Energy (1995a) has recently admitted that the earlier stages of the radiation experimentation projects were unorganized and operated without any real supervision. Part of the reason for this, according to the DOE (1995d, p. 20), is that in the beginning of the projects, "the task called for the creation of an enterprise far greater in scope and complexity than any single contemporary private industry on a pressing, almost desperate time schedule."

Like the many actors and institutions involved in U.S. human radiation experiments, there were also many different kinds of experiments conducted. Some of these studies turned out to be medically valuable, increasing the scientific knowledge of such diseases as cancer and diabetes. For example, studies were executed on the effects of iodine, zirconium, carbon, strontium, iron, copper, and phosphorus on general metabolism, thyroid production, arthritis, bone tumors, and glucose levels. Scores of other studies examined the effects of iron, hormone conversion, and carbon on human pregnancies, multiple myeloma, and liver disease.

Other studies were less noble in design, such as the nontherapeutic "nutrition" studies by MIT researchers in the 1940s and 1950s at the Fernald School. These studies involved exposing over a dozen developmentally disabled children to radioactive iron and calcium (U.S. Department of Energy, 1995a). Another general type of state-supported research that has been identified as ethically questionable are the numerous "Total-Body Irradiation" (TBI) experiments carried out at places such as the University of Cincinnati, Oak Ridge, and Baylor University's College of Medicine. These studies were in part funded by the Department of Defense for the purposes of gaining a better understanding of the effects of nuclear war on the human body. Other highly questionable experiments, in both legal and moral terms, include

a. 1961–65 MIT studies in which twenty elderly subjects were injected or fed radium and thorium;

b. 1953–57 Massachusetts General Hospital experiments that involved injecting uranium into patients with brain tumors;

c. 1961–63 University of Chicago and Argonne National Laboratory experiments involving 102 subjects who were fed radioactive fallout from the Nevada test site; and

d. 1950 studies at Columbia University in which twelve patients with terminal cancer were injected with radioactive calcium and strontium.

And the list could go on.

Legally questionable experiments have also been carried out through the testing of atomic and nuclear weapons. In experiments like those in the 1950s at the Nevada test site, hundreds of thousands of people were exposed to radioactive fallout from atomic and nuclear explosions. A recent study by the National Cancer Institute estimated that millions of children were exposed to radioactive iodine from the tests, and that perhaps 10,000 to 75,000 of them might develop thyroid cancer from this exposure (Neergaard, 1997). Downwinders, people living in areas downwind of the Nevada test site in Nevada, Arizona, and Utah, as well as military veterans who were forced to witness the explosions, have also experienced a disproportionate amount of illness traceable to atomic and nuclear weapons testing (Ball, 1986; Titus, 1986; U.S. House, 1990; 1986). Harmful consequences such as disproportionate levels of thyroid cancer also resulted from nuclear testing in the Marshall Islands, where sixty-six nuclear tests took place from 1946 to 1948 (U.S. House, 1994). These cases, like the cases of experimentation to be described later, represent criminal negligence on the part of the U.S. government and the AEC.

The Regulatory Environment

It is important to consider the nature and quality of state supervision of the U.S. human radiation experimentation program. There were AEC regulations protecting potential human subjects in the 1940s and 1950s, but these guidelines were never enforced over individual research organizations (Advisory Committee on Human Radiation Experiments, 1995; U.S. Department of Energy, 1995a). The first attempt by an AEC director to delineate human subject research guidelines was in 1947. AEC General Manager Carroll Wilson sent letters to Robert Stone and Stafford Warren, both researchers with the former Manhattan Project. These letters were not widely circulated by the AEC, and other than Stone and Warren, only some members of the Oak Ridge Laboratory, the AEC Advisory Committee for Biology and Medicine, and the AEC's Interim Medical Advisory Committee knew of their content. Wilson wrote in both letters that research should only proceed if there was reasonable hope that the experiment would have some sort of therapeutic effect, and that there should be documentary proof that the patient-subject was informed of the treatment and its possible effects (Advisory Committee On Human Radiation Experiments, 1995). The Wilson letters do indicate that the AEC was moving toward compliance with the Nuremberg Code's mandate of informed consent. What is problematic, however, is that the principles of consent and therapeutic value were never formally disseminated to research organizations and individual scientists. As the U.S. Department of Energy (1995a, p. 24) has recently stated, "The record does not show that the AEC distributed or enforced Wilson's policy." And the Advisory Committee on Human Radiation Experiments (1995, p. 91) has recently found that "Despite the fact that they were developed in response to a need for clarity in the way human research should be conducted, we have found little evidence of efforts to communicate or implement the rules stated by Wilson."

Wilson and the AEC Subcommittees do not appear to have treated the issues of subject consent and safety as a pressing matter (U.S. Department of Energy, 1995a). In fact, the AEC devoted most of its energies to the production of nuclear and atomic weapons. It is clear that the AEC failed to promote and mandate that its research be conducted in accordance with the Nuremberg Code. There is some debate about whether U.S. scientists, either working independently or for the government, considered the Nuremberg Code as a set of legal responsibilities that they were mandated to follow. Dr. Andrew Ivy was the Allies' medical expert in the Nuremberg trials, and his testimony indicates that indeed, there was global consensus among scientists that experiments should be conducted. (a) with full, informed consent, (b) for the good of society unprocurable by other means, and (c) only when it is deemed necessary.

The Advisory Committee on Human Radiation Experiments (1995) has recently examined the question of whether the Nuremberg Code was inculcated within the U.S. scientific community. After a thorough review of available documents, they concluded that "A minority of researchers and the organized medical profession did not exhibit a willingness to reconsider its responsibilities to patients in the burgeoning world of postwar clinical research." What we find very telling about this matter is that the U.S. government and its World War II allies were the main proponents of the establishment of international guidelines for the protection of human subjects. One would presume that the authors and creators of such a law would ensure that its own scientists act in a manner consistent with the law. This clearly was not the case.

It was not until the 1970s that the AEC, and then the Energy Research and Development Administration, developed a clear and codified set of ethical guidelines for human subject research. Based on the 1974 guidelines set forth by the Department of Health, Education, and Welfare (DHEW), which later developed into the National Research Act, the AEC as well as many state agencies such as the army, navy, and the air force finally (at least on paper) promulgated human subject guidelines consistent with the Nuremberg Code. This enormous thirty-year delay in the application of the Nuremberg Code is a prime example of U.S. indifference to the international law it so strongly supported (Simpson, 1995).

TWO CASE STUDIES OF HUMAN RADIATION EXPERIMENTATION

The Plutonium Injection Experiments

> The Advisory Committee is persuaded that these experiments were motivated by a concern for national security and worker safety. . . . However, with the possible exception of the polonium experiments, we believe that these experiments were unethical. . . . Two basic moral principles were violated—that one ought not use people as a mere means to the ends of others and that one ought not to deceive others. (Advisory Committee on Human Radiation Experiments, 1995, p. 267)

> The injection of lethal plutonium into healthy individuals showed a reckless disregard for human life by physicians, unfortunately, and others. (Dr. David Egilman, 1994, in testimony before the U.S. House of Representatives)

From 1945 to 1947, a series of Manhattan Project– and AEC–supported plutonium-injection studies were conducted on eighteen people. According to both primary and secondary documents, the studies were prompted by concerns over the exposure of large numbers of Manhattan Project and AEC workers to plutonium (Markey Report, 1986; U.S. Atomic Energy Commission, 1974; U.S. Department of Energy, 1984). Since there was only a rudimentary understanding of plutonium at this time (because animal tests were inconclusive), it was deemed necessary to conduct human experimentation. The subjects of the experiments were supposed to be individuals suffering from a disease or disorder that would allow them to live less than ten more years. This was not necessarily the case, however, and a few subjects were found to live significantly beyond this time.

Patients were injected with varying amounts of plutonium. The lowest injection is reported to be 4.5 micrograms, while the highest amounts of plutonium injected was 95 micrograms. It should be noted that while the Manhattan Project and the AEC were conducting these experiments to establish the maximum permissible amount of plutonium the body could withstand, AEC administrators estimated as early as 1945 that no more than 5 micrograms can be tolerated by the body (Advisory Committee on Human Radiation Experiments, 1995). Thus, the amount of plutonium injected into most of the subjects was clearly in excess of the conventional levels established for atomic weapons workers. It is also important to note that the very word "plutonium" was classified until 1947.

The first injection took place on April 10, 1945, at the Oak Ridge Hospital in Tennessee. Over the next two years, plutonium was intravenously injected into seventeen other people at the University of Rochester in New York, Billings Hospital at the University of Chicago, and the hospital of the University of California in San Francisco. Only one of the eighteen people involved in the experiments had given any kind of informed consent, and even this consent is somewhat questionable. This finding, confirmed by multiple sources (Advisory Committee on Human Radiation Experiments, 1995; Markey Report, 1986; U.S. Atomic Energy Commission, 1974, U.S. Department of Energy, 1995a), sheds considerable doubt on whether the Manhattan Project and the AEC conducted these experiments ethically and legally. Additionally, none of these experiments was conducted with the expectation that the patient-subject would benefit from the injections. Using governmental reports and de-classified documents, we can describe the experiments.*

The first plutonium guinea pig was fifty-three-year-old Ebb Cabe. Mr. Cabe was an Oak Ridge construction worker who did not fit the stated criteria for experimentation—he was physically healthy and suffered only from major fractures in his arm and legs as a result of an accident on the job. Cabe was injected with 4.7 micrograms of plutonium by Dr. Joseph Howland, an army doctor stationed at Oak Ridge. Dr. Howland reports that he was simply ordered to set up the injection, and was not instructed by his superiors to elaborate to his patient on the reasons for it. Apparently, the analysis of Cabe's urine and feces were not able to clear up the question of plutonium retention, and before physicians could inject him again, he mysteriously disappeared from the hospital. What is clear, however, is that Cabe did not know the nature of the experiment, nor that plutonium had been the substance injected into his body.

From April to December 1945, three cancer patients at the University of Chicago were selected for the plutonium experiments: A sixty-eight-year-old man suffering from cancer of the mouth and lung, a fifty-five-year-old woman with breast cancer, and a younger man (age undetermined) who was suffering from Hodgkin's disease. These three people were injected with the highest amount of plutonium in all of the experiments—95 micrograms. Again, there is no evidence of informed consent. Although E. R. Russell, a physician involved in the studies, reported in a 1974 fact-finding AEC study that while the patients were not expressly told that the substance was plutonium or that they would benefit from the procedure, physicians made some attempt to tell them that the experiment could be useful

---

*Much of the following is taken from a combination of sources, including the Advisory Committee on Human Radiation Experiments (1995), the U.S. Atomic Energy Commission (1974), the U.S. Department of Energy (1995a; 1995b; 1995d; 1984), and the Markey Report (1986).

for other people in the future (Advisory Committee on Human Radiation Experiments, 1995; U.S. Atomic Energy Commission, 1974). There is no corroborating evidence to support Russell's claim—in fact, the three patients' medical files contained no mention of the plutonium injections.

Eleven patients were injected with plutonium at the University of Rochester Hospital. Most of the patients were suffering from chronic, but not terminal, illnesses such as ulcers and heart disease. One patient was later found to be misdiagnosed and lived at least another twenty years. A telling comment about the position of scientists on the Rochester experiments is found in a 1946 letter from Wright Langham, an administrator, to Dr. Bassett, the primary physician at Rochester: "In case you should decide to do another terminal case, I suggest you do 50 micrograms instead of 5. . . . I feel reasonably certain that there is no harm in using larger amounts of material if you are sure the case is a terminal one" (Langham, 1946).

It is unclear how much plutonium was injected into each of the eleven patients. This is somewhat surprising, given our knowledge of the amounts administered in other experiments, but becomes understandable in light of another letter sent from Langham to Bassett. In this letter, Langham tells his colleague that the AEC head has asked him not to send in his data on the Rochester experiments because they might eventually end up in the medical files of the patients. Once again, as in past studies, there is no evidence that consent was given by the subjects in the Rochester study.

Three patients received plutonium injections at the University of California–San Francisco between 1945 and 1947. One of the subjects was Albert Stevens, a fifty-eight-year-old man thought to have advanced stomach cancer. After he had received months of plutonium injections, doctors found that in fact his tumor was benign; they considered paying him for his continued participation in the study. Records do not indicate whether payments were made or what happened to Stevens after the injections. Another subject was four-year-old Simeon Shaw, an Australian boy suffering from a rare form of bone cancer. Apparently the boy's parents had been advised by their physician that the California hospital could perhaps help his condition. This did not happen, and the boy died one year later. The California scientists later studied a portion of his tumor for its retention of plutonium. The third subject in California was a young African American man believed to be suffering from bone cancer. Unlike the other seventeen patients, it appears as though scientists did inform Elmer Allen that he was being injected with an "experimental substance." However, there is no evidence to indicate that the subject was told of the possible harmful effects of the injections, or that it was probably not going to be beneficial to his condition (Advisory Committee on Human Radiation Experiments, 1995).

The 1945–47 plutonium studies raise serious questions about whether the Manhattan Project, the AEC, and individual organizations and scientists conducted their experiments in a manner consistent with the Nuremberg Code. It is ironic that the U.S. government's successful attempt at Nuremberg to develop a codified international law on human experimentation was never applied to its own activities.* Granted, the Nuremberg medical trials were taking place during the period at which the plutonium experiments were occurring. But it is difficult to justify the state's deception of its own citizens when at the same time the United States was prosecuting individuals who had engaged in acts of a relatively similar nature.

The unethical behavior surrounding the plutonium experiments did not end in 1947. From 1950 to the early 1970s, researchers from Berkeley, Rochester, and Argonne Laboratory attempted to conduct a follow-up study on the subjects of the

---

*See Hunt (1991) for an examination of an equally disturbing instance of U.S. support for Nazi scientists who engaged in illegal human experiments.

1945–47 experiments. Recall that one of the criteria of the earlier studies was that the patients should suffer from a terminal condition that would make their survival beyond ten years very unlikely. However, as Dr. David Egilman (1994, p. 72) testified before the U.S. House Energy and Power Subcommittee, "The doses injected were potentially lethal, and I've reviewed the summary of the diagnoses. In my opinion, there is no way that physicians at the time could have thought those patients were terminal. Maybe three of those are questionable." Many subjects did live close to or well beyond ten years: One patient lived eleven years, another fourteen years, and four others lived at least twenty years after the injections (U.S. Department of Energy, 1984).

The follow-up study of two of the Rochester subjects was conducted until 1953. Both of the patients were still kept in the dark about the nature of the original experiments and the follow-up study. More startling, however, were the follow-up studies conducted through the University of Rochester Hospital and the Argonne Exhumation Project. The goals of the projects were to

> Uncover the post injection medical histories of all the subjects, obtain biological material from those still living, and exhume and study the bodies of those deceased in order to provide data on the organ contents at long times after the acquisition of plutonium. (Advisory Committee on Human Radiation Experiments, 1995, pp. 259–60)

The first component of the study, begun in 1973, was to admit three of the living subjects to the Rochester metabolic ward for more excretion studies. None of these patients was told that either the present research or the earlier studies were expected to have nontherapeutic results. In fact, one physician of the subjects did not tell her patient about the real reasons for the government's continuing interest in her because she thought the information might be damaging to the patient's health. Another physician expressly lied about the purpose of the follow-up study to his patient when he told the subject that the continuing medical attention was for the better understanding of the "treatment" he received in 1947. Thus, even after nearly thirty years since the original plutonium injections, the subjects were still being deceived and used as only "mere means" (Advisory Committee on Human Radiation Experiments, 1995).

The second part of the follow-up studies required the exhumation of deceased subjects. In a continuing criminal and unethical manner, the AEC in 1973 told the families of the deceased:

> The purpose of exhumation was to examine the remains in order to determine the microscopic distribution of residual radioactivity from past *medical treatment*, and that the subjects had received an unknown mixture of radioactive isotopes. (Advisory Committee on Human Radiation Experiments, 1995, p. 260) (Our emphasis)

This misleading explanation by the AEC is even more disturbing because it occurred in 1973, when not only was the Nuremberg Code universally recognized by nearly all scientists and governmental agencies, but when all governmental agencies were ordered to conduct their experiments only under the condition of informed consent. To further document the misleading nature of these follow-up studies, consider Argonne researcher Robert Rowland's suggestion:

> Please note that outside the Center for Human Radiobiology (at Argonne), we will *never* use the word plutonium in regard to these cases. "These individuals are of interest to us because they may have received a radioactive material at some time" is the kind of statement to be made, if we need to say anything at all. (Markey Report, 1986, p. 27)

In sum, the plutonium injection studies from 1945–47 and their follow-ups were conducted without any expectation of major medical benefit to the subjects. With the possible exception of one of the subjects in the Chicago study, no subject was informed of the nature, design, or purpose of the experiments.

Testicular Irradiation of Prisoners *

> In both Oregon and Washington, some subjects were not warned, warned only after enrolling in the experimental program, or inadequately warned that there was potential risk, albeit small, of testicular cancer. While it might not have been uncommon at the time for physicians to avoid using the term cancer with sick or even terminally ill patients for paternalistic reasons, such avoidance is harder to justify . . . in the case of healthy subjects who are participating in research that offers them no direct benefit. (Advisory Committee on Human Radiation Experiments, 1995, pp. 443–44)

From 1963 to 1973, 131 prisoners at the Oregon State Prison in Salem and the Washington State Prison in Walla Walla were subjects in a study to determine the effects of irradiation on the function of testes. There appear to be a number of reasons why the AEC was interested in this experiment. One project in which the Department of Defense was interested at the time was the development of an atomic-powered aircraft (U.S. Department of Energy, 1995a; 1995b). Pilots evidently were concerned about the effects of the machine on their fertility. Though the nuclear aircraft idea was eventually scratched, it is likely that this project laid the foundation for early governmental interest in the effects of radiation on the production of sperm (U.S. Department of Energy, 1995a).

---

*Most of the information included in this section on testicular irradiation was extracted from the sources identified in the footnote on p. 127, as well as from the U.S. Department of Energy (1976).

Another more likely antecedent to these studies was the desire to understand the effects of radiation on nuclear weapons production workers, astronauts, soldiers, and the general populace in the case of a nuclear war or accident. Also, as indicated in a memo to Melvin Koons, Contract Officer of the Oak Ridge Institute of Nuclear Studies, from K. L. England of the AEC, we also learn why prison administrators were initially interested in the study. According to England (1963, p. 2), "The use of inmates for medical research is looked upon most favorably by the wardens, since they feel any useful accomplishment by a penitentiary can in the end make it easier to secure adequate state funding." In sum, then, national security interests, perhaps with the professional and organizational rewards to be gained by human radiation experiments in prisons, served as fundamental motivations for the experiments.

As mentioned earlier, the AEC and many scientists felt that they needed to conduct experiments on human beings because animal tests had resulted in mixed findings. As Dr. Carl Heller (1973, p. 1), principal investigator of the Oregon study noted,

Man is different from other mammalian species in the kinetics of spermatogenesis. The cellular associations in the tubules are different, fewer generatives of spermatogytes exist between the stem cell and the mature sperm and the duration of spermatogenesis is longer in man than other species studied. Recovery time following irradiation is apparently prolonged in man as compared to other mammals. Thus, man is so different from other species studied, extrapolation of information obtained from the study of laboratory animals seems hazardous, if not impossible.

Illustrating further the nescience at the time, because of (unfounded) concerns of introducing "mutants" into the human gene pool by testicular irradiation, one condition of the experiments was that the subjects were to receive vasectomies at the termination of the study.

Technically stated, the goals of both the Oregon and Washington human radiation experiments were (a) to determine the minimal dosage of irradiation that causes temporary and permanent reduction and/or cessation of sperm production; (b) to determine the time required for recovery from any given dose; and (c) to determine the influence of radiation-produced testicular alteration upon hormone excretion (Heller, 1973, p. 1).

The medical results of the studies are easier to obtain than those from the plutonium experiments. The central findings were that (a) spermatogenesis in man is more radiosensitive than in rodents and recovery time is longer; (b) man is more radiosensitive to complete sterility than rodents; and (c) 100 rads caused sterility for nine to eighteen months, and 600 rads caused sterility for five or more years after the irradiation (U.S. Energy Research and Development Administrations, 1976).

Both studies were completely funded by the Atomic Energy Commission, with $1.12 million given to the Oregon researchers and $505,000 to the Washington investigators. Unlike the subjects in the plutonium-injection studies, the prisoners were informed of some, but clearly not all, of the effects of the irradiation (Advisory Committee on Human Radiation Experiments, 1995; Markey Report, 1986). There were no follow-up studies done on the original subjects because of lawsuits initiated by inmates. Indeed, the U.S. Attorney General even stepped in to eliminate the possibility of follow-ups because of the potential legal liability of the government.

Carl Heller, a renowned medical scientist, acted as the principal investigator for the Oregon study. Heller apparently found the possibility to engage in this kind of research quite attractive from a scientific perspective, since there was little in the way of a scientific literature on the subject. Much like the plutonium experiments, there was much to gain in the way of professional rewards for the individual scientists. The government, then, had a relatively easy task of finding individual researchers for their studies.

The Oregon experiments lasted from 1963 to 1971. Sixty-seven prisoners received testicular irradiation, with doses ranging from 8 to 640 rads. These doses were not and are not considered likely to produce cancer. Six of the inmates received a second irradiation, one inmate received a third irradiation, and one prisoner received eleven doses. There was no expected therapeutic value to the subjects—all subjects were in relatively good health and returned to their former state of fertility after the experiments. Inmates received $25 for each irradiation; and each prisoner was required to undergo a vasectomy at the conclusion of the research. A bonus of $25 was offered to the inmates to ensure their cooperation with this requirement. All of the inmates had vasectomies after the study was completed (U.S. Energy and Research Development Administration, 1976).

According to a paper Heller wrote with two of his colleagues, Daniel DiIaconi and Mavis Rowley, in 1973, prisoners learned of the experiment by word of mouth. Heller et al. (1973, pp. 7–8) provide us with the following examples of letters submitted to the scientists by inmates interested in the experiment:

a) "Dear Sir: I would like to talk with you as soon as possible about getting into the biopsy program. I have heard a lot about it and would like to sign up for it"

b) "I request to be interviewed in regards to your research program. I am particularly interested in being sterilized"

c) "I request to find out what a biopsy is as I may be interested"

d) "I request to talk with you about the biopsy program. I want to know what they do and so on. I am interested in doing this but I don't want to give an arm or something"

e) "I am doing a life sentence and due to the circumstances I would like to become involved into your research program as soon as possible. I would also like to become involved in the radiation program. I feel that if and when I get out I'll be too old to start another family" and

f) "I request to join your research program, as I am most interested in birth control."

There are many questions about the degree of informed consent the prisoners were able to give, and the degree to which a captive population can be said to participate in any study without coercion. There is little doubt that the prisoners agreed to participate in the study for the money—prisoners in Oregon could make only about 25 cents per day by working odd jobs. Moreover, there is considerable debate about the quality of information Dr. Heller and his associates gave to the prisoners about the experiments. Because there were eventually prisoner lawsuits over the experiments, we can garner some information from former inmates depositions. In one case, a prisoner said in 1976 that he had never been informed of the possibility of getting cancer from the irradiation. Many other prisoners repeated this story, and one reported that when they asked Dr. Heller about this, he replied that the possibility of cancer was only "one in a million" (Advisory Committee on Human Radiation Experiments, 1995, p. 426). Dr. Heller, in a deposition in the same year, said that he was afraid that if he used the term "cancer," the prisoners would be less likely to participate in the study, so when forced on the matter, he normally responded that there "might be the possibility of tumors of the testes" (Advisory Committee on Human Radiation Experiments, 1995, p. 426). In a study of the quality of information given by Dr. Heller, a governmental committee found:

> The acute risks of the exposures included skin burns, pain from the biopsies, testicular bleeding, and orchitis (testicu-

lar inflammation). . . . it appears that they (prisoners) were adequately informed about the possibility of skin burns, but perhaps inadequately, about the possibility of pain; informed about the possibility of bleeding only after 1970; and never informed about the possibility of orchitis. (Advisory Committee on Human Radiation Experiments, 1995, p. 426)

Dr. Heller was principally employed as a researcher with the Pacific Northwest Research Foundation (PNRF). According to Heller et al. (1973), a PNRF committee that monitored the progress of the research did briefly examine the ethics of the Oregon study. As indicated below, however, the committee seemed less concerned with the ethics of the experiment than the scientific progress of the research. According to Heller et al. (1973, p. 6):

In order to monitor experimental activities and provide expertise for unusual problems, advisory committees were selected and meetings were held. Discussion at the first meeting in November of 1963 centered around the proper handling of the volunteers. Subsequent meetings in December 1965, March 1967, and December 1967 were primarily to discuss various aspects of the work being done. . . . The first committee specifically polled officials giving permission for this project and personally visited the penitentiary to evaluate the knowledge and consent of inmate volunteers.

Thus, according to Heller, PNRF staff did in fact look into the ethical dimensions of the Oregon study, though we do not know the degree of interest or the quantity of time spent on the matter. Nevertheless, the primary and secondary evidence indicates that the Heller study was not forced by either the PNRF or the AEC to conduct the research in strict accordance with the Nuremberg Code (Advisory Committee on Human Radiation Experiments, 1995; Heller et al., 1973).

The testicular irradiation experiments in Oregon were terminated in 1973 when the administrator of the Oregon State Corrections Department concluded that prisoners could not consent freely to participate as subjects. Lawsuits were filed by nine former prisoners in 1976, originally requesting millions of dollars, in compensation for the lack of information given to them on the pain and suffering they would receive because of the experiment. Eventually, the lawsuit was settled out of court and the plaintiffs each received a paltry $2,215 in damages. But the fact that the AEC agreed to pay some prisoners for their suffering indicates that they perhaps accepted the fact that the study was not carried out in a manner consistent with the Nuremberg Code or extant AEC regulations (Advisory Committee on Human Radiation Experiments, 1995; U.S. Department of Energy, 1995a).

Like the subjects in the Oregon experiments, the Washington State prisoners were irradiated for the purposes of understanding the level at which workers, astronauts, and soldiers could feel reasonably safe working with and around nuclear and atomic weapons materials. Sixty-four inmates were irradiated in doses ranging from 7.5 to 400 rads. Like the Oregon subjects, prisoners had to agree to undergo a vasectomy at the conclusion of the research. Fifty-three of the subjects eventually received the vasectomies, while eleven declined the treatment.

Dr. C. Alvin Paulsen was principal investigator in the experiments, which lasted from 1963 to 1973. One of the main differences from the Oregon experiments was that Paulsen placed a bulletin board notice inside the prison to attract subjects. A portion of the advertisement read:

> The project concerns effects of radiation on human testicular function and the results of the project will be utilized

in the safety of personnel working around atomic steam plants, etc. . . . It is possible that those men receiving higher doses may be temporarily, or even permanently, sterilized. (Advisory Committee on Human Radiation Experiments, 1995, p. 430)

And in quotation marks at the end of the advertisement, was the following: "This is a simple procedure under local anesthesia. It is not a very painful procedure." This kind of information, which at best might be misleading or considered incomplete, is the only information available on the conduct and quality of Dr. Paulsen's study. This study, however, like Dr. Heller's, did not comply with the spirit and letter of the Nuremberg Code, which requires subjects to have full knowledge of the effects of the experiments (Markey Report, 1986). Moreover, the question again arises about the ability of inmates to freely engage in human experiments. Dr. Audrey Holliday, chief of research at the Washington Department of Corrections, sent a letter to Dr. William Conte, the general director of corrections in Washington, which began the downfall of the research. She wrote,

There is no doubt but that the prison setting is an ideal setting for this type of research. . . . I suppose concentration camps provided ideal settings for the research conducted in them. . . . If, in fact, non-inmates were to volunteer in the substantial numbers of persons Dr. Paulsen needs, then I would have less qualms about offering up a captive population for this research. (Advisory Committee on Human Radiation Experiments, 1995, p. 432)

Eventually, Dr. Conte was forced to put an end to the studies, in part because of an order by the Department of Corrections Human Rights Review Committee, which saw the experiment as inconsistent with the standards of the Nuremberg Code. This is quite contrary to the claims by the AEC throughout its tenure that all of their studies had been conducted legally and ethically. For example, when both the Oregon and Washington studies were first approved, the AEC, for the most part, took a hands-off approach to the matter of informed consent. In 1963, when the prisoner studies were first developing, a memo from AEC Chief of Radiation Sciences K. L. England (1963, p. 2) includes the following observation:

> we are not aware of any statute or law that would prohibit or inhibit this experiment. . . . We recognize that it is most important to fully inform the inmate of all details of the experiment including the intention to irradiate to complete sterilization in some cases and then accept those volunteers who agree in writing.

The irony here is that the Nuremberg Code is ignored in two ways. First, and most disturbing, it is not even acknowledged that the code holds domain over these experiments. Secondly, the matter of consent is not addressed within the context of the other guidelines of the code, namely, the illegality of an experiment conducted under duress, coercion, or fraud. As we have detailed, there is little question that the Oregon and Washington prisoner experiments violated the spirit and substance of the Nuremberg Code, whether or not the individual researchers and state managers considered it applicable to their activities.

ANALYSIS

Human radiation experiments have been sponsored by the U.S. government since the dawn of the atomic age. The vast majority of these experiments were illegal under international law since they violated the Nuremberg Code. To conclude this chapter, we highlight some of the factors that shaped these violations.

Once again we start with the issues of goals and means. We

have already established that the United States became increasingly dependent on nuclear weapons as an instrument of foreign policy as a result of the outcome of World War II and the development of the Cold War. Given their dependence on these weapons to protect and advance the "vital interests" of the United States, political leaders and the various government agencies that made up the nuclear national security state needed to know as much as possible about the effects of nuclear weapons, particularly radiation effects. A willing and able scientific community conducting human radiation experiments was a means to that end.

The motivation of the scientists involved in the experiments was surely to contribute to the advancement of scientific knowledge and to the national security of their country. But there were also more tangible rewards to be gained by these scientists such as the prestige of receiving major government research grants, publication in scholarly works,* and other academic rewards such as tenure and promotion. Given these inducements and the silence of the government sponsors on the ethical and legal issues involved, it is perhaps easier to see why so many researchers became involved in these illegal and unethical experiments.

As we documented above, there was little in the way of regulation or oversight concerning human radiation experiments. The government did not require the contracted scientists to follow the guidelines of the Nuremberg Code and did little to monitor their activity. The general culture of secrecy within the nuclear national security state and its agencies shielded these experiments from any congressional or public scrutiny. With virtually no social control mechanisms operat-

---

*The AEC and its successors funded a number of research projects that allowed scientists to publish their findings in scholarly journals. For a detailed list of these articles, see Advisory Committee on Human Radiation Experiments (1995), U.S. Department of Energy (1995a), and U.S. Energy and Research Development Administration (1976).

ing, and a veil of secrecy surrounding their actions, it is not hard to see why government agencies pressured to achieve organizational goals related to the development of nuclear weapons used the most effective and efficient means available, even if they violated international law.

There can be little doubt that the people responsible for the studies knew that their behavior was highly questionable, if not illegal, under international law. Buried documents, officially classified memos, and the outright policy to keep subjects ignorant of the nature of the research lend considerable support to this position. Furthermore, we have presented primary evidence that there were direct orders given by administrators within the various energy agencies to quash any use of the term "human subjects" because of the potential legal trouble that could, and in some cases did, result. All of this indicates a gross lack of concern by the U.S. government for the applicable and universally accepted principles created at Nuremberg.

7

Explaining and Controlling the Crimes of the Nuclear State

To this point we have described and analyzed various crimes of the nuclear state. In this final chapter we present a more general theoretical explanation of these crimes and outline some approaches to controlling them. Theory, in its simplest form, is the attempt to answer the question "why?" Here we ask the question "why?" with regard to the U.S. state crimes we have described.

THEORIES OF ORGANIZATIONAL CRIME

Social-Psychological Theories

The social-psychological level of analysis examines individuals within a group context. A prime example of this more "micro" approach is Sutherland's differential association theory, one of the first theories to be applied to white-collar crime. Sutherland was attempting to develop a general theory of crime by arguing that criminal behavior is learned through interaction within intimate, personal groups and in isolation from those who define such behavior unfavorably. A person in a particular situation will engage in criminal behavior if the weight of the favorable definitions exceeds the weight of the unfavorable definitions. Partial support for differential association as a theory was found by a number of criminologists in the early decades of white-collar crime research (Albanese, 1982; Clinard, 1946; Cressey, 1950; Geis, 1967; Lane, 1953).

A more recent individually based "general theory" of crime that has also been applied to white-collar crime is that of Hirschi and Gottfredson (1987; 1989). They argue that all behavior results from the pursuit of self-interest and that the essence of criminality lies in individuals' low self-control (Gottfredson and Hirschi, 1990). Crimes are events in which force or fraud is used to achieve immediate gratification, and criminals are those with faulty socialization and weak ties to the community and thus low self-control. However, a number of criminologists have questioned the applicability of this "general theory" of crime to the reality of organizational crime (Friedrichs, 1996; Reed and Yeager, 1996; Steffensmeier, 1989).

While some important insights can be derived from theories at the micro level, their failure to incorporate the organizational and structural levels of analysis is a major weakness. Theories that focus only on social-psychological variables cannot adequately explain why organizations as social actors violate the law. As Schrager and Short (1978, p. 410) observe, "Preoccupation with individuals can lead us to underestimate the pressures within society and organizational structure, which impel those individuals to commit illegal acts." Thus, macrosociological rather than individual levels of explanation are necessary to explain organizational crimes.

Organizational Theories

Organizational theorists argue that the organization itself should be central to the analysis of organizational crime (Albanese, 1982; Clinard and Yeager, 1980; Ermann and Lundman, 1978b; Finney and Lesieur, 1982; Gross, 1978; 1980; Kramer, 1982; Scrager and Short, 1978; Vaughan, 1982; 1983). The development of this organizational perspective was hailed as an important theoretical advance in the general field of white-collar crime. Indeed, Braithwaite (1985, p. 3) has even asserted that "theoretical progress began only in the late 1970s when the individualistic theory spawned by the Sutherland tradition was rejected in favor of applying organizational theory paradigms to the phenomenon."

The organizational theorists argue that "there is built into the very structure of organizations an inherent inducement for the organization itself to engage in crime" (Gross, 1978, p. 56). Most of these theorists borrow heavily from Merton's theory of anomie, a traditional criminological theory, to develop their approach (Passas, 1990). Organizations, they argue, are strongly goal oriented and concerned with performance, while norms governing the means to achieve these goals may be weak or absent. Thus, legitimate means to achieve goals may be unavailable or blocked in some way. The emphasis on goal attainment, combined with blocked legitimate means, may induce "strain" and compel organizations to "innovate" and use illegitimate means to achieve their goals. As Finney and Lesieur (1982, p. 270) state, "barriers to the attainment of desired performance may generate such severe strain that agents resort to illegal solutions." It should be noted that these barriers to the attainment of goals can be internal to the organization (that is, defective standard operating procedures) or come from various sources in the external environment.

In addition to performance pressure and strain, organizational crime also seems to depend on two other factors. First, pursuing goals through illegitimate means depends on the availability of those illegal means. Organizational crime is more likely to occur when illegitimate opportunities for achieving the organization's goals are available to organizational actors (Braithwaite, 1989). Second, the social control environment also plays a role in fostering organizational crime. As Finney and Lesieur (1982, p. 275) note, "whether or not a strong performance orientation and operating problems lead to crime depends also on the operationality of various social controls."

The anomie tradition focusing on the organizational level of analysis has been the most widely used theoretical perspective in the field of organizational crime and has generated much research (Passas, 1990). This perspective will be central to the integrated theoretical approach we present in this chapter.

The Structural Level: Theories of Political Economy

A third perspective on organizational crime operates on the structural or institutional level of analysis. This level deals with the larger social structure and the major social institutions of society. Political and economic institutions in particular, and the interrelationships between them, merit special attention in an effort to explain organizational crime (Barnett, 1981; Box, 1983; Chambliss, 1988; 1989; Messerschmidt, 1986; Michalowski, 1985; Young, 1981).

The primary assumption of this perspective is that the structure of corporate capitalism, as an economic system, provides the major impetus toward organizational crime. Capitalism provides the major incentives for organizations to use illegitimate means to achieve profit or create the conditions under which capital accumulation may take place. In many instances this perspective extends the Mertonian strain model by considering how the mode of material production generates illegal activity. As Barnett (1981, p. 5) argues, corporate crime occurs "when management chooses to pursue corporate goals through circumvention of market constraints in a manner prohibited by the state." The state may also commit crimes as it attempts to create the optimum conditions for the worldwide operation of its transnational corporations.

Michalowski (1985) has suggested that the various criminal acts that are usually referred to as white-collar crime can be brought together in the more theoretically informed concept of "crimes of capital." Crimes of capital are "socially injurious acts that arise from the ownership or management of capital or from the occupancy of positions of trust in institutions designed to facilitate the accumulation of capital" (Michalowski, 1985, p. 314). According to Michalowski, corporate crime, state crime, organized crime, and occupational crime all arise from the particular forms of social relations associated with the processes of capital accumulation, concentration, and centralization. It should be noted that this applies as much to accumulative institutions in socialist societies as to those in capitalist ones.

The organizational perspective and the political economy perspective have many similarities. The major unit of analysis in both is the organization, whether the corporation or the state. Both place great emphasis on the concept of organizational goals. Both analyze the problems organizations can encounter as they attempt to achieve goals through legitimate means. Both argue that organizations will turn to illegal means under circumstances of strain and both note the importance of social control mechanisms in controlling organizational crime. The critical difference is the way in which the political economy perspective stresses the shaping and constraining influence of the broader historical, institutional structure of society on organizational behavior.

Integrated Theories of Organizational Crime

In recent years there have been several attempts to develop a more integrated theoretical explanation of organizational crime. Coleman (1987), using the concept of the "culture of competition," argues that criminal behavior results from a coincidence of appropriate motivation and opportunity. Braithwaite (1989) asserts that the key to an integrated theory of organizational crime is the notion of "differential shaming": the shaming that can come from an organizational culture of compliance can deter crime, while the shaming from a subculture of resistance to regulatory law can encourage crime.

Passas (1990, p. 173) starts with Merton's anomie theory and argues that "when situations calling for problem departures from institutional norms persist, social interactions foster the development of deviant but effective patterns of action, along with (subcultural) rationalizations 'justifying' them." Once these practices are in place and become legitimate, more of them can occur even in the absence of any structural pressures (Passas, 1990). Finally, in a monumental work, Vaughan (1996) analyzes the "normalization of deviance" with regard to the *Challenger* launch decision, providing dramatic insights into the link between culture and individual choice concerning organizational misconduct. We will draw on all of these theoretical efforts in developing our integrated framework.

AN INTEGRATED FRAMEWORK FOR THE STUDY OF ORGANIZATIONAL CRIME

Figure 1 outlines an integrated theoretical framework that is intended to help analyze various forms of organizational crime. This framework links the three levels of analysis we noted above with three catalysts for action. These catalysts for action or core concepts are (a) motivation or performance emphasis, (b) opportunity structure, and (c) the operationality of social control. This framework is designed to indicate the key factors that will contribute to or restrain state crime at each intersection of a catalyst for action and a level of analysis.

The framework is based on the proposition that criminal behavior at the organizational level results from a coincidence of pressure for goal attainment, availability and perceived attractiveness of illegitimate means, and an absence or weakness of social control mechanisms. These three concepts are interdependent. It will be difficult to address them separately without the risk of overgeneralizing or minimizing their impor-

Figure 1
Catalysts for Action

Levels of Analysis	Motivation	Opportunity Structure	Operationality of Control
Institutional environment (History, political economy, culture)	Culture of competition Economic pressure Organizational goals Performance emphasis	Availability of legal means Obstacles & constraints Blocked goals/strain Availability of illegal means Access to resources	International reactions Political pressure Legal sanctions Media scrutiny Public opinion Social movements
Organizational (Structure and process)	Corporate culture Operative goals Subunit goals Managerial pressure	Instrumental rationality Internal constraints Defective SOPs Creation of illegal means Role specialization Task segregation Computer, telecommunication, and networking technologies Normalization of deviance	Culture of compliance Subcultures of resistance Codes of conduct Reward structure Safety & quality control procedures Communication processes
Interactional (Face-to-face interaction, individual action)	Socialization Social meaning Individual goals Competitive individualism Material success emphasis	Definitions of situation Perceptions of availability & attractiveness of illegal means	Personal morality Rationalizations & techniques of neutralization Separation from consequences Obedience to authority Group think Diffusion of responsibility

tance. Nevertheless, we will discuss each catalyst for action separately and then fuse them together in order to interpret the data from the case studies.

Individuals and organizations have varying kinds of goals and varying degrees of commitment to achieving those goals. Some theorists have argued that the greater the emphasis on goal attainment, the more likely the resulting behavior will be criminal. Given this assumption, we would expect that if an individual is highly goal oriented, works in an organization that evaluates performance strictly on goal attainment, in a society whose cultural and institutional structures emphasize achievement above all else, then the chances for organizational misconduct are high.

Most crimes involve both motivation and opportunity. All the motivation in the world to act in a particular way means little if the opportunity to carry out that action is not available. The second catalyst for action in the framework directs attention to the opportunity structure of means that organizations and their agents might use to achieve organizational goals. A frequent proposition in the organizational crime literature is that when legal means to achieve goals are blocked or for some reason unavailable, then organizational actors will turn to illegal means if they are available. In studying state or corporate crime, therefore, it is important to describe the differential distribution of both legal and illegal means to accomplish organizational goals.

Even if legal means are available, agents may still decide to use illegal means in the pursuit of their goals if the norms or cultural definitions of the organization support them. Illegal means may also be selected if they are more effective and efficient. Organizations tend to operate with instrumental rationality. That is, they seek out and employ those means that are the most likely to achieve organizational goals, which are usually pregiven and not open for discussion or reflection. Means that are the most effective and efficient in achieving these established goals of the organization are particularly likely to be selected in the absence of strong social controls.

The operationality of social-control mechanisms and agents is the third core concept in the model. Social forces exist at all three levels of analysis, exerting pressure on organizations and organizational actors and checking their efforts to select illegal means to goal attainment. At the structural level, various forms of legal sanctions, both domestic and international, could be imposed by criminal justice or other governmental regulatory bodies. Domestic or international public opinion could pressure offending organizations. Scrutiny from the mass media, social movement organizations, or citizen watchdog groups could exert social-control influence. At the organizational level, internal cultures of compliance may regulate the behavior of organizational actors. Finally, at the individual level, strong ethical standards may be an important bulwark against involvement in opportunities for organizational crime.

A highly motivated organization with easy access to illegal means of goal attainment may be blocked from committing an organizational crime by the operation of one or more of these social control mechanisms. In analyzing the crimes of the nuclear state or any organizational crime, it is important to take into account the existing forces of social control, their effectiveness, and the ability of the organization to evade or neutralize these control mechanisms.

EXPLAINING CRIMES OF THE NUCLEAR STATE

Having outlined the integrated model, the next step is to fuse the case studies with the theory. We ended each of the case study chapters with a brief analysis highlighting specific factors the data indicated as important for understanding why these illegal acts occurred. We proceed by reviewing each core concept on all the different levels of analysis as they pertain to each of the three case studies.

Motivation

All of the nuclear crimes we have described were committed to advance the broader structural and institutional goals of the United States. These goals were the protection of national security and the pursuit of vital economic and political interests. From the atomic race with Nazi Germany to the Cold War with the Soviet Union, U.S. policy makers sought to obtain atomic and nuclear weapons to reduce U.S. vulnerability to foreign attack. These weapons could be used not only to protect the United States, but also to deter a Soviet attack in Western Europe and protect other allies around the world.

Nuclear weapons could also be used to project U.S. power around the world to maintain empire, the U.S.–dominated global economic and political system of the post–World War II years. As Gerson (1995, p. xiii) observes: "My studies and work taught me that nuclear weapons have been used to expand and maintain the U.S. 'sphere of influence' since the bombings of Hiroshima and Nagasaki, notwithstanding the use of the Cold War with the Soviet Union as the sole rationale for the nuclear arms race." This "nuclear umbrella" has served to back up U.S. foreign policy initiatives and military interventions in the Third World to ensure that those nations would continue to play their assigned service role of providing resources, cheap labor, markets, and investment opportunities for U.S.–based transnational corporations (Chomsky, 1995).

As these structural goals were pursued, institutional practices and ideological beliefs developed to provide further support for the nuclear state. World War II began the development of a huge military-industrial complex in the United States that was assured ongoing support by decisions to keep the U.S. economy on a war footing in order to face the presumed Soviet threat. This complex consists of defense contractors, the Department of Defense, members of Congress, the weapons laboratories, and defense industry labor unions. Although not generally mentioned in the literature except through its connection to the Department of Defense, the president and his administration should also be considered a component of the military-industrial complex. These components interact with each other on a regular basis and are interrelated in the process of developing and producing nuclear weapons and other military items. Each component of what Marullo (1993) calls the "iron pentagon" gains significant benefits from high levels of military spending and U.S. nuclear weapons policies. Thus, each component of the complex has a vested economic or political interest in keeping the Pentagon's budget high and American nuclear policies in place. The institutional goals and practices of the military-industrial complex, therefore, provide further motivations for the nuclear national security state and its crimes.

To these structural and institutional goals we must add ideological goals and beliefs. While socialist political movements and parties were quite strong in the United States in the early part of the century (Zinn, 1995), powerful anticommunist sentiment also existed. Anticommunist beliefs, militarism, and support for empire grew, eventually giving rise to the Cold War and growing stronger because of it. These cultural forces mixed easily with the modern conservative movement in the United States that gained great strength in the 1970s and 1980s. Anticommunism, "peace through strength," high military budgets, and an aggressive, interventionist foreign policy to defend the American empire became staples of the Republican party from Goldwater to Reagan to Gingrich, and part of the worldview of many Americans, including many liberal and conservative Democrats. These strongly held militaristic beliefs and goals of conservative ideology also provide critical support for the nuclear state and its policies.

Nuclear extortion, environmental contamination from the

nuclear production process, and human radiation experiments are all products of the effort to protect national security and pursue the vital economic and political interests of empire by the United States. These were the most important structural and institutional level motivations for the crimes detailed in this study.

The goals of the specific organizations involved in these illegalities can also be clearly delineated. The AEC and its successors were mandated to produce weapons and to discern the effects of atomic and nuclear radiation on human beings. These were the only goals of these organizations and thus their budgets and very survival depended on goal attainment. We described earlier the significant pressure placed on the AEC for the production of accurate and timely information and materials relating to nuclear weapons.

The Eisenhower and Nixon administrations also were pursuing their organizational goals by attempting to end the Korean and Vietnam Wars through the threat of atomic and nuclear weapons. The data indicate that Eisenhower and Nixon were at times absolutely consumed with ending the wars that the U.S. public also wanted terminated as quickly as possible. The organizational-level motivations for crimes of the nuclear state, then, were to end two unpopular wars in a timely manner, to produce nuclear materials and warheads, and to assemble data on nuclear energy and radiation.

Although our focus is on organizational and structural levels of analysis, we have found that individual actors involved in the illegalities were rewarded for helping state agencies to achieve their goals. The scientists and administrators involved in human radiation experiments were rewarded (normally by way of sustained employment and research grants) for their contribution to the attainment of organizational goals. Eisenhower and Nixon each had much to gain by successfully ending the respective wars that they had inherited. Each had pledged during a political campaign to end the war, and each envisioned his future reputation and political stature as some-how related to his atomic and nuclear threats. In sum, the key individuals involved in these illegalities achieved individual goals and some measure of personal success by participating in state crimes.

Opportunity Structures

At the end of World War II, the opportunity structure for the U.S. government to achieve its national security and foreign policy goals was practically limitless. The United States came out of the war as the number one military power in the world, the number one economic power in the world, and the undis-puted political leader in global affairs. The major competitors to U.S. dominance were militarily defeated and/or physically and economically devastated by the war. Although the Soviet Union would soon offer a significant challenge in some ways, the United States occupied the preeminent position in world affairs in the immediate postwar years.

Given the great power and resources of the United States, the government encountered both a favorable opportunity structure and a great deal of freedom from international con-trols as it pursued its structural goals. With all the legitimate opportunities available, why then did the United States use the illegitimate means we have described as crimes of the nuclear state? As we have noted, many organizations turn to illegal means to achieve organizational goals when legal means are blocked in some way. The United States was not able to achieve victory in either Korea or Vietnam by using conven-tional military power or diplomacy, and in both cases a stale-mate ensued. Political and ideological competition from the Soviet Union also constrained U.S. actions in various parts of the world. Allied opposition to the use of atomic weapons in Korea and domestic protest over Vietnam blocked Eisenhower and Nixon from actually using weapons of mass destruction in their respective conflicts. Significant time pressures to end the wars, to produce nuclear warheads, and to obtain scientific knowledge about radiation were perceived to limit the choice of means available in some situations.

These factors certainly reduced some of the legal means that government agencies had available to them to accomplish their goals, but that does not fully explain the criminality that occurred. We argue that a more likely explanation for these crimes is that the available illegal means were more effective and efficient in achieving structural and organizational goals.

To our knowledge, this possibility has not been discussed in the literature before. Could it be that some organizations choose to use illegal means because those means are judged, in terms of instrumental rationality, to be more effective and efficient in accomplishing given organizational goals than available legal means? As Jackall (1980, p. 355) points out, "The rational/technical ethos of bureaucracy transforms even those issues with grave moral import into practical concerns." The instrumental rationality of the organizational form itself may be partially responsible for the crimes we have described. Again, Jackall (1980, p. 356) notes, "The very rationality which makes bureaucratic structures effective administrative tools seems to erode moral consciousness."

On the structural level, then, it is clear that opportunities to commit nuclear crimes were readily available owing to a variety of government policies and resources. National security acts shielded atomic and nuclear organizations, as well as presidential administrations, from internal legal obstacles, public pressures, and social outrage. Sufficient resources were always provided for the production and experimentation programs, while presidential administrations held principal power and discretion over the use of and threat to use nuclear weapons. In sum, with all the power and resources available, and using instrumental reasoning, U.S. policy makers decided to use the most effective and efficient means to achieve their foreign policy objectives regardless of their legality under international law.

On the organizational level of analysis, we have found that the policies and guidelines of the Department of Energy and its predecessors were focused only on the goal of production. Again, the most effective means, regardless of legality, were employed by nuclear-related state agencies. Legitimate and illegitimate means for goals attainment were defined not in reference to law but in relationship to how they helped further the mission of the organization. A method was illegitimate if it could not produce expected results; a method was legitimate when it did. Since structural opportunities existed for unleashed methods, it should therefore not surprise us to see the same type of phenomenon on the organizational level. The nuclear production complex was never forced to engage in methods that were inconsistent with their organizational goals; neither was the AEC or its successors limited in their methods to manufacture knowledge about the physiology of atomic and nuclear energy. The Eisenhower and Nixon administrations also had more than enough opportunity to threaten the use of atomic and nuclear weapons to end the wars. The resources and information were available, as was the discretion. On an organizational level of analysis, actors and agencies were free to use the most effective methods to pursue their goals. The most effective means available, however—threatening to use nuclear weapons, disposing of radioactive waste in the ground and water, performing experiments without informed consent—were generally illegal.

Individual researchers, scientists, administrators, and employees appear to have had as much opportunity as their organizations to pursue the most effective means to complete their role requirements. In the case of human radiation experimentation, the scientists were never ordered to conduct their research in accordance with the Nuremberg Code. They were given every opportunity, and perhaps every reason, not to compromise their scientific agendas by infusing matters of ethics and morality. The same is true with nuclear weapons production complex employees and administrators. As individuals, Nixon and Eisenhower (along with their advisors) were limited only by their consciences and the degree to which they could hide their questionable behavior from important control audiences.

On the interactional level, it is also important to point out that many of these individuals were socialized into organizational cultures where these illegal means were defined as appropriate and necessary (in part because they were effective and efficient). Part of the social learning that goes on in most organizational settings is the acquisition of rationalizations that justify why things are done the way they are. In addition, organizational agents are often quite isolated from alternative social definitions of the means or methods they are expected to use. This was especially true in the extreme culture of secrecy that prevailed in agencies of the nuclear state.

Social Control

On a structural level, we can envision no greater lack of social control than in the case of the U.S. nuclear weapons program. Secrecy has been the rule, and only in the last few years have we witnessed any movement on the part of the government to open the program up for public and scholarly scrutiny. From the Manhattan Project to the present, it has been exceptionally difficult, if not impossible, for outside audiences to gain accurate information concerning government actions regarding such things as nuclear and atomic tests, human radiation experimentation, the consequences of warhead production, or the multiple instances of nuclear extortion. Though there indeed have been some important antinuclear weapons social movements and journalistic exposés on the state's nuclear programs, they did not gain the level of prestige or power necessary to mobilize a major change in the policy of secrecy. The most common result of critical queries into the weapons program has been the dismissal or neutralization of such charges by the state, mostly through invoking the language of "national security." The legacy of secrecy has successfully shielded the nuclear state from outside scrutiny and public accountability for years.

Focusing on the role of social control at the organizational and institutional level of analysis, we also find that the Department of Energy and its predecessors were not closely monitored by any independent body. Left to achieve its organizational goals without fear of publicity or legal challenges, the production complex employed methods that, if discovered by a significant social group outside the complex, would be considered not only criminal but probably unconscionable. The same is true for the human experimentation program, which operated for years by both tacitly and explicitly deceiving subjects and classifying potentially injurious information. As we have noted, the operationality of social control over the Eisenhower administration by international audiences appeared to force him to forgo actually dropping atomic bombs on North Korea, and instead only to threaten their use. Here we see the potential of external groups to force adjustments in a state's policy. The Nixon administration also experienced the effects of social disapproval by a significant sector of the domestic populace over the use of nuclear weapons against North Vietnam, and readily admitted that the choice only to threaten the use of the weapon was a result of this public opinion. In both cases, adverse public reactions and protest were able to block the actual use of weapons of mass destruction, which was a monumental accomplishment. In each case, however, another, lesser form of crime, nuclear extortion, replaced the blocked action.

Individuals within the various organizations had much to lose by not remaining complicit in the nuclear crimes. Data suggest that the reward structure had little to offer those concerned with environmental safety, the consent of research subjects, or the losing of a war. It is appropriate to note that rationalizations were employed by various actors to make their harmful activities more acceptable to themselves and others.

Theoretical Conclusion

Our integrated framework is intended to shed some light on the possible causes of crimes of the U.S. nuclear state. We have attempted to explain threats to use atomic and nuclear weapons in the Korean and Vietnam Wars, the contamination of the environment through the production of nuclear weapons, and illegal human radiation experiments, by employing a theoretical model that integrates different levels of analysis. Interpreting nuclear crimes on the structural, organizational, and individual levels of analysis appears to provide a sufficiently comprehensive understanding of the multiple dimensions of motivation, opportunity, and social control. Most instances of state criminality are probably not caused by one factor or social process alone, and theories that assume singular causes are often limited in their explanatory power. We take the position that in order to develop a more complete understanding of nuclear crimes and state criminality, we must pay close attention to the interrelationship between the macrosociological and microsociological worlds (Vaughan, 1996), and how these spheres operate and interact with the core concepts of motivation, opportunity, and control. Crimes of the nuclear state are indeed a product of the specific goals, opportunities, and lack of controls over the state in general, its nuclear-related organizations, and those employed within those organizations. Extremely high goal orientation with an almost unlimited choice of methods to achieve those goals results in conditions conducive to state criminality. Combine this with limited social controls, and the stage is set for a criminal outcome. These are precisely the conditions that led to crimes of the American nuclear state.

We hope this model offers a starting point for a better understanding of the phenomenon of state criminality. The model has limitations, of course. Theory and data are impossible to disconnect in any true sociological, scholarly venture. So, like the scores of other inductively generated theories, ours must be applied to other instances of organizational crime in order to gauge its explanatory power. Since the model draws from the existing literature, though, portions of our theoretical approach have already been tested, and for the most part have been found to play significant roles in the genesis and persistence of organizational crime in general, and state criminality in particular. We believe that the model will prove applicable to other instances of organizational misconduct as well.

CONTROLLING NUCLEAR CRIMES AND STATE CRIMINALITY

Any theory of crime contains implications for the social control of criminal behavior. Having developed a theoretical explanation for the crimes of the nuclear state, we turn our attention in this brief final section to the broader issue of how to control nuclear crimes and state criminality.

Reducing the Motivation for State Criminality

In our theoretical analysis we argued that the primary motivation for the crimes of the nuclear state came from the structural goals of U.S. foreign policy in the mid-twentieth century. Reducing the motivation for nuclear crimes would require changing these structural, institutional, and ideological goals. This will be a difficult task; the forces behind these goals are strong. Even the end of the Cold War and the dissolution of the Soviet Union brought about only limited changes in the nuclear national security state or the military budget. Terrorists, rogue states, and nuclear outlaws quickly replaced the Soviet Union as the primary threat to national security. Michael Klare (1995) has documented how U.S. policy makers quickly adopted the "rogue doctrine" and developed a new formal strategic policy to ensure that the United States was capable of fighting more than one major regional war, such as the Gulf War against Iraq, at the same time. The goals of protecting national security from military threats, defending the U.S. empire and its "vital interests" in the Third World, maintaining the defense budget and the benefits of the military-industrial complex, and supporting conservative ideological beliefs are all kept in place with this new strategic doctrine despite the massive changes that have taken place in the world.

To reduce the motivations for nuclear crimes and other forms of state criminality we need to redefine national security and the "vital interests" of the United States, reduce the power of the military-industrial complex, and challenge the militarism of conservative ideology. All of these objectives depend on the greater democratization of U.S. society, that is, the greater public participation of U.S. citizens in the major political and economic decisions that affect our lives.

The redefinition of national security and U.S. vital interests must be based on a realistic assessment of the world security environment. As Klare (1995, p. 214) points out, "Such an assessment would rank global chaos as the greatest future threat, followed by the potential for escalation in regional disputes, the uncontrolled spread of ethnic and sectarian strife, and the prospect of mass migration from disintegrating states." In the face of these threats, Klare asserts, American security policy should have as its primary goal the amelioration of global discord and violence. Other goals that follow from this would be the resolution of existing conflicts, the negotiated settlement of disputes between states and peoples, the reduction of the international arms trade, the strengthening of international peacekeeping efforts, and the promotion of economic development in the Third World (Klare, 1995, p. 214).

The adoption of these national security goals would lead to a new military strategy and a restructuring of U.S. military forces. The military would now have to be "trained and equipped for a wide variety of peacemaking and crisis control activities—including multilateral peacekeeping operations, enforcement of U.N. arms embargoes, and humanitarian aid and rescue—in addition to traditional military activities" (Klare, 1995, p. 228). Such a military posture should lead to a denuclearization of U.S. forces and, in turn, foster nuclear nonproliferation among Third World states. If these objectives could be achieved, then the total elimination of all weapons of mass destruction becomes a realistic possibility.

Another consequence of the adoption of a new national security policy and a new military posture would be a reduction in the power and influence of the military-industrial complex. If the U.S. military is restructured to focus on peacekeeping operations and international crisis control, and there is a substantial reduction in nuclear weapons systems, the military budget can be reduced by a large amount. With a much smaller and reoriented Pentagon, and the development of a national economic conversion plan, the military-industrial complex would shrink and the political pressure it exerts would lessen considerably.

It will not be possible to develop new security goals or reduce the military-industrial complex, however, if the power of transnational corporations to shape public policy in the United States is not curtailed. Transnational corporations seeking resources, markets, cheap labor, and investment opportunities have long driven the U.S. empire and its foreign policy. Defense industry corporations seeking profits in supplying the Pentagon and fostering the international arms trade have been the dominant component of the military-industrial complex.

To protect their interests and secure their profits these corporations have exercised disproportionate power over state policy. Massive campaign financing, revolving doors between corporate and government positions, funding of conservative think tanks, and increasing media monopolization are some of the ways in which this corporate influence is obtained.

Unless a powerful social movement based on a broad coalition of labor, environmental activists, peace and justice supporters, women's and minority advocates, and religious groups arises to challenge this corporate-state system and democratize political decision making in the United States, none of the changes we have discussed will happen. Such a social movement faces both structural and cultural obstacles. On the one hand, the material resources and political structures to organize such a movement are limited at best. Additionally, ideological beliefs about empire, foreigners, militarism, and the proper role of government in society also make it difficult to bring together a broad coalition dedicated to the peace and security goals discussed above.

Friedrichs (1996) has argued that the first step in any program for a more effective response to white-collar or organizational crime of any type is to raise consciousness of the problem. Perhaps this book, and the literature it has reviewed, can help to elevate the level of consciousness about state crime in our society.

Reducing Opportunity and Increasing Controls

In addition to the issue of motivation, our theoretical model pointed to the importance of looking at opportunity structures and social control mechanisms in understanding state criminality. To prevent or reduce organizational crime in general, access to legitimate opportunities must be opened up, access to illegitimate opportunities must be closed down, and effective measures of social control must be put into operation.

With regard to crimes of the nuclear state, we pointed out

that with all the power and resources available to government agencies and following a logic of instrumental rationality, U.S. policy makers tended to use the most effective and efficient means to achieve their structural and organizational goals.

Given this situation, the operationality of social control mechanisms takes on added significance. As we noted above, a variety of social-control agents could become involved in the effort to reduce governmental crime. International agencies such as the United Nations and the International Court of Justice can direct sanctions and the power of public opinion at offending states. Regional organizations like the Organization of American States can take certain actions against and put public pressure on transgressing member-states. The ICJ decision on the illegality of nuclear weapons and the signing of the Comprehensive Test Ban Treaty in September 1996 are two recent examples of international bodies exerting some measure of social control, however limited, over the nuclear states of the world.

Within the United States, greater public and governmental support for the United Nations, the ICJ, and other international organizations will be essential. Checks and balances in the government itself could be utilized to control deviant acts by other government agencies. Congressional oversight and regulatory sanctions, for example, can be imposed. In addition, independent and investigative media could play an important role in exposing government crime. Private watchdog organizations and citizen groups, such as those created by Ralph Nader, can also monitor governmental agencies and exert the pressure of public opinion.

With regard to the nuclear crimes we have discussed, the great wall of secrecy that the U.S. government imposed in the name of national security on all atomic and nuclear projects made it extremely difficult for any of these control agents to have much effect. Only when the shroud of secrecy is penetrated can state crimes be exposed and sanctioned. The redefinition of national security and new structural goals would lessen the need for government agencies and officials to cloak their actions in secrecy. Beyond that, the American people must insist on greater democratic accountability on the part of their government. That will happen only if the broad-based social movement mentioned above can be organized to challenge the existing corporate-state system.

These forms of domestic social control, however, would have to be linked to a variety of international movements and control efforts to have the greatest impact. Only an invigorated United Nations and an empowered World Court, along with respected and effective regional organizations, could truly sanction and control state criminality like the crimes of the nuclear state. The worldwide movement to abolish weapons of mass destruction remains perhaps the last best hope to save the world from future nuclear crimes, including the greatest crime of all, the destruction of the planet.

REFERENCES

Abas, B. (1989). Rocky Flats: A mistake from day one. *The Bulletin of the Atomic Scientists* (October): 19–24.

Acheson, D. (1969). *Present at the creation: My years in the State Department.* New York: Norton.

Adams, S. (1961). *First-hand report: The story of the Eisenhower administration.* New York: Harper.

Aday, D. P. (1990). *Social control at the margins: Towards a general understanding of deviance.* Belmont, Calif.: Wadsworth.

Advisory Committee on Human Radiation Experiments. (1995). *Final report.* Washington, D.C.: U.S. Government Printing Office.

Akehurst, M. (1987). *A modern introduction to international law.* London: Allen and Unwin.

Albanese, J. S. (1982). *Organizational offenders.* Niagara Falls, N.Y.: Apocalypse.

Alverez, R. (1990). Personal communication.

Arbatov, G., and Oltmans, W. (1983). *The Soviet viewpoint.* New York: Dodd, Mead.

Arkin, W., and Fieldhouse, R. (1985). *Nuclear battlefields: Global links in the arms race.* Cambridge, Mass.: Ballinger.

Aulette, J. R., and Michalowski, R. (1993). Fire in Hamlet: A case study of state-corporate crime. In *Political crime in contemporary America: A critical approach*, ed. K. D. Tunnell, 171–206. New York: Garland.

Bailey, S. D. (1972). *Prohibitions and restraints in war.* London: Oxford University Press.

Ball, H. (1986). *Justice downwind: America's atomic testing in the 1950s.* New York: Oxford University Press.

Barak, G. (1990). Crime, criminology, and human rights: Towards an understanding of state criminality. *Journal of Human Justice* 2: 1–28.

———. (1991). *Crimes by the capitalist state: An introduction to state criminality.* Albany: State University of New York Press.

Barnett, H. (1981). Corporate capitalism, corporate crime. *Crime and Delinquency* 27: 4–23.

Bassiouni, C. (1992). *Crimes against humanity in international criminal law.* Boston: Martinus Nijhoff.

Baudot, M., et al. (1977). *The historical encyclopedia of World War II.* New York: Facts on File.

Baxter, R. R. (1953). The role of law in modern warfare. *Proceedings of the American Society of International Law* 47: 90–98.

Becker, T., and Murray, V. G., eds. (1971). *Government lawlessness in America.* New York: Oxford University Press.

Berding, A. (1965). *Dulles on diplomacy.* Garden City, N.Y.: Doubleday.

Berman, H. (1972). *Soviet criminal law and procedure.* Cambridge: Harvard University Press.

Berman, H., and Baker, J. (1982). *Soviet strategic forces: Requirements and responses.* Washington, D.C.: Brookings Institution.

Bialer, S., and Mandelbaum, M. (1988). *The global rivals.* New York: Alfred A. Knopf.

Bilder, R. (1984). Nuclear weapons and international law. In *Nuclear weapons and the law*, ed. M. Feinrider and A. Miller, 131–55. Westport, Conn.: Greenwood.

Blechman, B., and Kaplan, S. (1978). *Force without war: U.S. armed forces as a political instrument.* Washington, D.C.: Brookings Institution.

Bledsoe, R. L., and Boczek, B. A. (1987). *The international law dictionary.* Santa Barbara: ABC-CLIO.

Borchard, E. (1946). The atomic bomb. *American Journal of International Law* 40: 161–65.

Box, S. (1983). *Power, crime, and mystification.* London: Tavistock.

Boyle, F. (1983). *The criminality of nuclear weapons.* Santa Barbara: Nuclear Age Peace Foundation.

———. (1984). International lawlessness in the Caribbean basin. *Crime and Social Justice* 21–22: 37–57.

———. (1985). *World politics and international law.* Durham: Duke University Press.

———. (1987). The lawlessness of nuclear deterrence. *Swords and Plowshares* 2: 8–9.

———. (1989). The hypocrisy and racism behind the formulation of U.S. human rights foreign policy: In honor of Clyde Ferguson. *Social Justice* 16(1): 71–93.

Braithwaite, J. (1984). *Corporate crime in the pharmaceutical industry.* London: Routledge and Kegan Paul.

———. (1985). White collar crime. *Annual Review of Sociology* 11: 1–25.

———. (1989). Criminological theory and organizational crime. *Justice Quarterly* 6: 333–58.

Builder, C., and Graubard, M. (1982). *The international law of armed conflict: Implications for the concept of assured destruction.* New York: RAND Corporation Publishers.

Bundy, M. (1988). *Danger and survival: Choices about the bomb in the first fifty years.* New York: Random House.

Center for Defense Information. (1988). Nuclear bomb factories: The dangers within. *Defense Monitor* 17(4): 1–8.

———. (1989). Defending the environment? The record of the U.S. military. *Defense Monitor* 18(6): 1–6.

Chambliss, W. (1988). *On the take: From petty crooks to presidents.* Bloomington: Indiana University Press.

———. (1989). State-organized crime. *Criminology* 27: 183–208.

———. (1995). Commentary. *Society for the Study of Social Problems (SSSP) Newsletter* (Winter).

Chomsky, N. (1987). *On power and ideology.* Boston: South End Press.

———. (1988). *The culture of terrorism.* Boston: South End Press.

———. (1993). *Year 501: The conquest continues.* Boston: South End Press.

———. (1995). *World orders old and new.* New York: Columbia University Press.

Citizens' Petition to State and Federal Authorities. (1991). Brief in Support of the Nuremberg Campaign.

Clarfield, G., and Wiecek, W. (1984). *Nuclear America: Military and civilian power in the United States.* New York: Harper & Row.

Clark, R. (1992). *The fire this time: U.S. war crimes in the Gulf.* New York: Thunder's Mouth Press.

Clinard, M. B. (1946). Criminological theories of violations of wartime regulations. *American Sociological Review* 11: 258–70.

Clinard, M., and Quinney, R. (1973). *Criminal behavior systems: A typology.* New York: Holt, Rinehart, & Winston.

Clinard, M., and Yeager, P. (1980). *Corporate crime.* New York: Free Press.

Cloward, R. (1959). Illegitimate means, anomie, and deviant behavior. *American Sociological Review* 30: 5–14.

Cochran, T. B. (1988). U.S. nuclear weapons production: An overview. *Bulletin of the Atomic Scientists* (January–February): 12–17.

Cochran, T. B., Arkin, W. M., and Hoenig, T. (1984). *Nuclear weapons databook: U.S. nuclear forces and capabilities.* Cambridge, Mass.: Ballinger.

Coffee, J. (1977). Beyond the shut-eyed sentry: Toward a theoretical view of corporate misconduct and effective legal response. *Virginia Law Review* 63: 1099–1278.

Cohen, A. K. (1977). The concept of criminal organization. *British Journal of Criminology* 17: 97–111.

———. (1990). Criminal actors: Natural persons and collectivities. In *New directions in the study of justice, law, and social control,* Arizona State University School of Justice Studies, 101–25. New York: Plenum.

Coleman, J. S. (1974). *Power and the structure of society.* New York: W. W. Norton.

———. (1982). *The asymmetric society.* Syracuse: Syracuse University Press.

Coleman, J. W. (1987). Toward an integrated theory of white-collar crime. *American Journal of Sociology* 93: 406–39.

———. (1994). *The criminal elite: The sociology of white collar crime.* 3rd ed. New York: St. Martin's Press.

Congressional Budget Office. (1994). *Cleaning up the DOE's nuclear weapons complex.* Washington, D.C.: Congressional Budget Office.

Conner, T. (1990). Nuclear workers at risk. *Bulletin of the Atomic Scientists* (September): 24–29.

Cressey, D. R. (1950). The criminal violation of financial trust. *American Sociological Review* 15: 738–43.

————. (1953). *Other people's money: A study in the social psychology of embezzlement.* Glencoe, Ill.: Free Press.

————. (1989). The poverty of theory in corporate crime research. In *Advances in criminological theory,* ed. W. S. Laufer and F. Adler, 1: 31–55. New Brunswick, N.J.: Transaction Publishers.

Denzin, N. (1989). *The research act.* 3rd ed. Englewood Cliffs, N.J.: Prentice-Hall.

Egilman, D. (1994). Statement before the U.S. Congress, House. Committee on Energy and Commerce. Subcommittee on Energy and Power. Washington, D.C.: U.S. Government Printing Office.

Eisenhower, D. D. (1963). *Mandate for change: 1953–1956: The White House years.* New York: Doubleday.

Ellsburg, D. (1981). Fall to mutiny. In *Protest and Service,* ed. F. P. Thompson and D. Smith, i–xxviii. New York: Monthly Review Press.

Emery, R. (1990). Personal communication, December.

England, K. L. (1963). Memo to Melvin Koons. Oak Ridge Research Division, Box 454.

Ermann, M. D., and Lundman, R. J. (1978a). Deviant acts by complex organizations: Deviance and social control at the organizational level of analysis. *Sociological Quarterly* 19 (Winter): 55–67.

————. (1978b). *Corporate and governmental deviance: Problems of organizational behavior in contemporary society.* 1st ed. New York: Oxford University Press.

————. (1987). *Corporate and governmental deviance: Problems of organizational behavior in contemporary society.* 3rd ed. New York: Oxford University Press.

————. (1996). *Corporate and governmental deviance: Problems of organizational behavior in contemporary society.* 5th ed. New York: Oxford University Press.

Falk, R. (1983). Toward a legal regime for nuclear weapons. *McGill Law Journal* 28: 519–30.

————. (1989). United States foreign policy as an obstacle to realizing the rights of peoples. *Social Justice* 16(1): 57–69.

Falk, R., Kolko, G., and Lifton, R. J. (1971). *Crimes of war.* New York: Vintage.

Feagin, J., Orum, A., and Sjoberg, G. (1991). *A case for the case study.* Chapel Hill: University of North Carolina Press.

Feinrider, M. (1982). International law as the law of the land: Another constitutional constraint on the use of nuclear weapons. *Nova Law Journal* 7: 103–28.

Ferencz, B. (1980). *An international criminal court—a step toward world peace: A documentary history and analysis*. New York: Oceana Publications.

Finer, S. E. (1977). *Five constitutions*. Brighton, Eng.: Harvester Press.

Finney, H. C., and Lesieur, H. R. (1982). A contingency theory of organizational crime. In *Research in the sociology of organizations*, ed. S. B. Bacharach, 255–99. New York: Random House.

Frankel, M. (1989). *Out of the shadows of night: The struggle for international human rights*. New York: Delacorte Press.

Frappier, J. (1984). Above the law: Violations of international law by the U.S. government from Truman to Reagan. *Crime and Social Justice* 21: 1–36.

Friedman, L. (1972). *The law of war: A documentary history*. New York: Random House.

Friedrichs, D. (1985). The nuclear arms issue and the field of criminal justice. *Justice Professional* 1: 5–9.

———. (1995). State crime or governmental crime: Making sense of the conceptual confusion. In *Controlling state crime*, ed. J. Ross, 53–79. New York: Garland.

———. (1996). *Trusted criminals: White collar crime in contemporary society*. Belmont, Calif.: Wadsworth.

Fujita, H. (1982). First use of nuclear weapons: Nuclear strategy versus international law. *Kansai University Review of Law and Politics* 3: 57–86.

Galliher, J. F. (1989). *Criminology: Human rights, criminal law, and crime*. Englewood Cliffs, N.J.: Prentice-Hall.

Geis, G. (1967). The heavy electrical equipment antitrust cases of 1961. In *Criminal behavior systems*, ed. M. Clinard and R. Quinney, 139–50. New York: Holt, Rinehart, & Winston.

Geis, G., and Meier, R. (1977). *White-collar crime: Offenses in business, politics, and the professions*. New York: Free Press.

Gelb, L. H. (1991). A nuclear ripoff. *New York Times*, June 26, p. 15.

Georgiou, P. (1973). The goal paradigm and notes toward a counter paradigm. *Administrative Science Quarterly* 18: 291–310.

Gerson, J. (1995). *With Hiroshima eyes: Atomic war, nuclear extortion and moral imagination*. Philadelphia: New Society Publishers.

Giddens, A. (1987). *The nation state and violence*. Berkeley: University of California Press.

Glaser, B. G., and Strauss, A. L. (1967). *The discovery of grounded theory: Strategies for qualitative research*. New York: Aldine de Gruyter.

Glueck, S., and Glueck, E. (1950). *Unraveling juvenile delinquency*. Cambridge: Harvard University Press.

Gottfredson, M. R., and Hirschi, T. (1990). *A general theory of crime*. Stanford: Stanford University Press.

Goulden, J. C. (1984). *Korea: The untold story*. New York: Times Books.

Grabosky, P. N. (1989). *Wayward governance: Illegality and its control in the public sector*. Sidney: Australian Institute of Criminology.

Gramsci, A. (1973). *Letters from prison*. New York: Harper & Row.

Gray, C. (1977). *The geopolitics of the nuclear era*. New York: Crane Russak.

Gray, P. (1995). *Official use only: Ending the secrecy in the U.S. nuclear weapons complex*. San Francisco: Tides Foundation.

Green, G. S. (1990). *Occupational crime*. Chicago: Nelson-Hall.

Gross, E. (1978). Organizational crime: A theoretical perspective. In *Studies in symbolic interaction*, ed. N. Denzin, 55–85. Greenwich, Conn.: JAI Press.

———. (1980). Organizational structure and organizational crime. In *White-collar crime: Theories and research*, ed. G. Geis and E. Stotland, 52–67. Beverly Hills: Sage.

Habermas, J. (1973). *Legitimation crisis*. Boston: Beacon Press.

Haldeman, H. R. (1978). *The ends of power*. New York: Times Books.

Hall, R. (1987). Organizational behavior: A sociological perspective. In *Handbook of organizational behavior*, ed. J. W. Lorsch, 112–31. Englewood Cliffs, N.J.: Prentice-Hall.

Halperin, M. H.; Berman, J., Borosage, R., and Marwick, A. (1976). *The lawless state: Crimes of the U.S. intelligence agencies*. New York: Penguin Books.

Harding, R. (1983). Nuclear energy and the destination of mankind: Some criminological perspectives. *Australian and New Zealand Journal of Criminology* 16: 81–93.

Harrison, J. (1982). *The endless war: Fifty years of struggle in Vietnam.* New York: Free Press.

Haynes, V. D. (1997). Grand jury clamors to break its silence in Rocky Flats case. *Chicago Tribune,* C edition, p.4.

Haywood, O. G. (1947). Memo to Dr. Fidler. Oak Ridge Research Division, Box 603.

Heller, C., DiIaconi, D., and Rowley, M. (1973). *Protection and welfare of prison volunteers: Policies followed throughout a 17-year medical research program.* Seattle: Pacific Northwest Research Foundation.

Henkin, L. (1991). The use of force: Law and U.S. policy. In *Right v. might: International law and the use of force,* ed. J. T. Swing, 37–70. New York: Council on Foreign Relations Press.

Henry, S. (1991). The informal economy: A crime of omission by the state. In *Crimes by the capitalist state: An introduction to state criminality,* ed. G. Barak, 289–311. New York: State University of New York Press.

Herman, E. S. (1982). *The real terror network: Terrorism in fact and propaganda.* Boston: South End Press.

Hersch, S. (1983). *The price of power: Kissinger in the Nixon White House.* New York: Summit Books.

Hirschi, T. (1969). *Causes of delinquency.* Berkeley: University of California Press.

Hirschi, T., and Gottfredson, M. R. (1987). Causes of white-collar crime. *Criminology* 25: 949–74.

———. (1989). The significance of white-collar crime for a general theory of crime. *Criminology* 27: 359–71.

Hodges, J. (1991). Personal communication, January.

Holloway, D. (1983). *The Soviet Union and the arms race.* New Haven: Yale University Press.

Hopkins, A. (1978). The anatomy of corporate crime. In *Two faces of deviance: Crimes of the powerless and powerful,* ed. P. R. Wilson and J. Braithwaite, 79–91. Brisbane, Australia: University of Queensland Press.

Hunt, L. (1991). *Secret agenda: The United States government, Nazi scientists, and Project Paperclip.* New York: St. Martin's Press.

International Court of Justice (1996). *The legality of the threat or use of nuclear weapons* (Request for advisory opinion submitted by the General Assembly of the United Nations). General List, No. 95, Advisory Opinion of 8 July.

Jackall, R. (1980). Crime in the suites. *Contemporary Sociology* 9 (May): 354–58.

Johns, C. J., and Johnson, P. W. (1994). *State crime, the media, and the invasion of Panama*. Westport, Conn.: Praeger.

Kaku, M., and Axelrod, D. (1987). *To win a nuclear war: The Pentagon's secret war plans*. Boston: South End Press.

Karnow, S. (1983). *Vietnam: A history*. New York: Viking Press.

Kauzlarich, D. (1994). Epistemological barriers to peacemaking criminology. *Peace Review* 6(2): 165–70.

———. (1995). A criminology of the nuclear state. *Humanity and Society* 19(3): 37–57.

———. (1997). Nuclear weapons on trial: The battle at the International Court of Justice. *Social Pathology* 3 (Fall): 157–64.

Kauzlarich, D., and Kramer, R. C. (1993). State-corporate crime in the U.S. nuclear weapons production complex. *Journal of Human Justice* 5(1): 4–28.

———. (1995). The nuclear terrorist state. *Peace Review* 7: 333–38.

Kauzlarich, D., Kramer R. C., and Smith, B. (1992). Toward the study of governmental crime: Nuclear weapons, foreign intervention, and international law. *Humanity and Society* 16(4): 543–63.

Kearns, D. (1973). *Lyndon Johnson and the American Dream*. New York: Harper & Row.

Kelman, H. C., and Hamilton, V. L. (1989). *Crimes of obedience*. New Haven: Yale University Press.

Khrushchev, N. (1970). *Khrushchev remembers*. Boston: Little, Brown.

Kissinger, H. (1979). *The White House years*. Boston: Little, Brown.

Klare, M. (1995). *Rogue states and nuclear outlaws: America's search for a new foreign policy*. New York: Hill and Wang.

Kovel, J. (1983). *Against the state of nuclear terror*. Boston: South End Press.

Kramer, R. C. (1982). The debate over the definition of crime: Paradigms, value judgments, and criminological work. In *Ethics, public policy, and criminal justice*, ed. F. Elliston and N. Bowie, 33–58. Cambridge, Mass.: Oelgeschlager, Gunn & Hain.

———. (1992). The space-shuttle Challenger explosion: A case study of state-corporate crime. In *White-collar crime reconsidered*, ed. K. Schlegel and D. Weisburd, 241–66. Boston: Northeastern University Press.

Kramer, R. C., and Kauzlarich, D. (1997). The International Court of Justice opinion on the illegality of the threat or use of nuclear weapons: Implications for criminology. Paper presented at the annual meeting of the American Society of Criminology, November 20, San Diego.

Kramer, R. C., and Marullo, S. (1985). Toward a sociology of nuclear weapons. *Sociological Quarterly* 26: 277–92.

Kramer, R. C., and Michalowski, R. J. (1990). Toward an integrated theory of state-corporate crime. Paper presented at the annual meeting of the American Society of Criminology, November, Baltimore.

Krater, J. (1991). Personal communication, January.

Kuhn, T. (1962). *The structure of scientific revolutions*. Chicago: University of Chicago Press.

Kull, S. (1988). *Minds at war: Nuclear reality and the inner conflicts of defense policymakers*. New York: Basic Books.

LaFeber, W. (1991). *America, Russia and the cold war*. 2nd ed. New York: McGraw-Hill.

Laird, R. F., and Herspring, D. R. (1984). *The Soviet Union and strategic arms*. London: Westview Press.

Lamperti, J. (1984a). Government and the atom. In *The nuclear almanac: Confronting the atom in war and peace*, ed. J. Dennis, 67–79. Reading, Mass.: Addison-Wesley.

———. (1984b). Nuclear weapons manufacture. In *The nuclear almanac: Confronting the atom in war and peace*, ed. J. Dennis, 69–81. Reading, Mass.: Addison-Wesley.

Lane, R. E. (1953). Why businessmen violate the law. *Journal of Criminal Law* 14: 151–56.

Langham, W. (1946). Memo to Samuel Bassett. Department of Energy. ACHRE No. DOE-121294-D-4, 1.

Laqueur, W., and Rubin, B. (1989). *The human rights reader*. Rev. ed. New York: Meridian.

Lauterpacht, H. (1952). The revision of the law of war. *British Year-book of International Law* 29: 360–82.

Lawyers' Committee on Nuclear Policy. (1984). Statement on the illegality of nuclear weapons. In *Toward nuclear disarmament and global security*, ed. B. K. Weston, 146–51. New York: Lawyers' Committee on Nuclear Policy.

———. (1990). *Statement on the illegality of nuclear weapons*. New York: Lawyers' Committee on Nuclear Policy.

Lens, S. (1982). *The bomb*. New York: Lonestar Books.

Lieberman, J. K. (1972). *How the government breaks the law*. Briar Cliff Manor, N.Y.: Stein and Day.

Lifton, R. J., and Mitchell, G. (1995). *Hiroshima in America: Fifty years of denial*. New York: Grosset and Putnam.

Lincoln, W. B. (1968). *Documents in world history: 1945–1967*. San Fransisco: Chandler.

Luken, T. (1989). *Statement before the U.S. Congress, House*. Committee on Energy and Commerce. Subcommittee on Transportation and Hazardous Materials. Environmental crimes at DOE's nuclear weapons facilities. 101st Cong., 1st sess. Washington, D.C.: U.S. Government Printing Office.

Makhijani, A., Hu, H., and Yih, K., eds. (1995). *Nuclear wastelands: A global guide to nuclear weapons production and its health and environmental effects*. Cambridge: MIT Press.

Markey Report (1986). *American nuclear guinea pigs: Three decades of radiation experiments on U.S. citizens*. Report prepared by the Subcommittee on Energy Conservation and Power. Committee on Energy and Commerce, U.S. House of Representatives: Washington, D.C.: U.S. Government Printing Office.

Marullo, S. (1993). *Ending the cold war at home: From militarism to a more peaceful world order*. New York: Lexington Books.

Matthews, R., and Kauzlarich, D. (1997). The FAA and Valujet: A case study in state-facilitated crime. Paper presented at the annual meeting of the American Society of Criminology, San Diego, November 20.

McCaughan, E. (1989). Human rights and peoples' rights: An introduction. *Social Justice* 16: 1–7.

McNaught, L. W. (1984). *Nuclear weapons and their effects*. London: Brasseys Press.

Merrick, G. B. (1987). *Statement before the U.S. Congress, House*. Committee on Energy and Commerce. Subcommittee on Transportation and Hazardous Materials. Environmental crimes at DOE's nuclear weapons facilities. 101st Cong., 1st sess. Washington, D.C.: U.S. Government Printing Office.

Merton, R. (1938). Social structure and anomie. *American Sociological Review* 3: 672–82.

Messerschmidt, J. (1986). *Capitalism, patriarchy, and crime*. Totowa, N.J.: Rowman and Littlefield.

Meyrowitz, E. L. (1981). The status of nuclear weapons under international law. *Guild Practitioner* 38: 65–82.

———. (1990). *Prohibition of nuclear weapons: The relevance of international law*. Dobbs Ferry, N.Y.: Transnational Publishers.

Michalowski, R. J. (1985). *Order, law and power*. New York: Random House.

Michalowski, R. J., and Kramer, R. C. (1987). The space between laws: The problem of corporate crime in a transnational context. *Social Problems* 34: 34–53.

Miller, A., and Feinrider, M. (1984). *Nuclear weapons and the law*. Westport, Conn.: Greenwood Press.

Miller, R. I. (1975) *The law of war*. Lexington, Mass.: Lexington Books.

Mobilization for Survival. (1989). *Banning the bombmakers: Challenging nuclear weapons production*. New York: Mobilization for Survival Fund.

Mohr, L. B. (1973). The concept of organizational goal. *American Political Science Review* 67 (June): 470–81.

Mohr, M. (1988). International humanitarian law and the law of armed conflict: Its relevance to the nuclear challenge. In *Lawyers and the nuclear debate*, ed. M. Cohen and M. E. Govin, 83–90. Ottawa: University of Ottawa Press.

Moore, B. (1966). *Social origins of dictatorship and democracy*. Boston: Beacon Press.

Morris, R. (1977). *Uncertain greatness*. New York: Harper & Row.

Myren, R. *Law and justice*. Pacific Grove, Calif.: Brooks/Cole.

National Academy of Sciences. (1987). *Safety issues at the defense pro-*

duction reactors: A report to the department of energy. Washington, D.C.: National Academy Press.

Needleman, M. L., and Needleman, C. (1979). Organizational crime: Two Models of Criminogenesis. *Sociological Quarterly* 20: 517–28.

Neergaard, L. (1997). 50s fallout posed threat to thyroids. *Philadelphia Inquirer,* August 2.

Newhouse, J. (1989). *War and peace in the nuclear age.* New York: Alfred A. Knopf.

Nicaragua v. United States of America. ICPREP. 14 (1986).

Nixon, R. M. (1978). *The memoirs of Richard Nixon.* New York: Grosset and Dunlap.

———. (1985). *No more Vietnams.* New York: Arbor House.

Nuremberg Campaign (1990). *Violation of international law.* Ocscoda, Mich.: Nuremberg Campaign.

O'Brien, W. V. (1961). Some problems of the law of war in limited nuclear warfare. *Military Law Review* 14: 1–27.

Office of Technology Assessment (1972). *The effects of nuclear war.* Washington, D.C.: U.S. Government Printing Office.

———. (1991). *Complex cleanup: The environmental legacy of nuclear weapons production.* Washington, D.C.: U.S. Government Printing Office.

Olshansky, S. J., and Williams, R. G. (1988). Culture shock at the weapons complex. *Bulletin of Atomic Scientists* (September): 29–33.

Passas, N. (1990). Anomie and corporate deviance. *Contemporary Crises* 14: 157–78.

Pentagon Papers (1971). *The secret history of the Vietnam War.* ed. Neil Sheehan. New York: Bantam Books.

———. (1973). *The Defense Department history of United States decision-making on Vietnam.* Gravel Edition. Boston: Beacon Press.

Perdue, W. D. (1989). *Terrorism and the state: A critique of domination through fear.* Westport, Conn.: Praeger.

Perkins, R. (1991). *The ABCs of the Soviet-American nuclear arms race.* Pacific Grove, Calif.: Brooks/Cole.

Perrow, C. (1961). The analysis of goals in complex organizations. *American Sociological Review* 26 (December): 688–99.

Perrucci, R., and Potter, H. R. (1989). *Networks of power: Organizational actors at the national, corporate, and community levels.* New York: Aldine de Gruyter.

Porter, J. W. (1986). *Statement before the U.S. Congress, House*. Committee on Government Operations. Subcommittee on Environment, Energy, and Natural Resources. Review of DOE's compliance with environmental laws in managing its hazardous and mixed radioactive-hazardous wastes. 99th Cong., 2d sess. Washington, D.C.: U.S. Government Printing Office.

Powaski, R. E. (1987). *March to Armageddon: The United States and the nuclear arms race, 1939 to the present*. New York: Oxford University Press.

Public papers of the president of the United States: Harry S. Truman. (1950). Washington, D.C.: U.S. Government Printing Office.

Public papers of the president of the United States: Dwight D. Eisenhower. (1952). Washington, D.C.: U.S. Government Printing Office.

Public papers of the president of the United States: Richard Nixon. (1971). Washington, D.C.: U.S. Government Printing Office.

Public Papers of the president of the United States: Richard Nixon. (1974). Washington, D.C.: U.S. Government Printing Office.

Radioactive Waste Campaign. (1988). *RWC report*. New York: Radioactive Waste Campaign.

Reed, E., and Yeager, P. C. (1996). Organizational offending and neoclassical criminology: Challenging the reach of a general theory of crime. *Criminology* 34: 357–77.

Reicher, D. W. (1986). *Statement before the U.S. Congress, House*. Committee on Energy and Commerce. Subcommittee on Transportation and Hazardous Materials. Environmental crimes at DOE's nuclear weapons facilities. 101st Cong., 1st sess. Washington, D.C.: U.S. Government Printing Office.

Reicher, D. W., and Scher, S. J. (1988). Laying waste to the environment. *Bulletin of Atomic Scientists* (January–February): 29–31.

Rhodes, R. (1986). *The making of the atomic bomb*. New York: Simon & Schuster.

Riggs, R. E., and Plano, J. C. (1988). *The United Nations: International organization and world politics*. Pacific Grove, Calif.: Brooks/Cole.

Roberts, A., and Guelff, R. (1982). *Documents on the laws of war*. Oxford: Clarendon Press.

Roebuck, J., and Weeber, S. (1978). *Political crime in the United States*. New York: Praeger.

Ross, J. I. (1995). *Controlling state crime: Toward an integrated structural model*. New York: Garland.

Saleska, M., and Makhijani, I. (1990). Hanford cleanup: Explosive solution. *Bulletin of Atomic Scientists* (October): 14–20.

Schlegel, K., and Weisburd, D. (1992). *White-collar crime reconsidered*. Boston: Northeastern University Press.

Schrager, L. S., and Short, J. F. (1978). Toward a sociology of organizational crime. *Social Problems* 25: 407–19.

Schwartzenberger, G. (1958). *The legality of nuclear weapons*. London: Stevens & Sons.

Schwendinger, H., and Schwendinger, J. (1970). Defenders of order or guardians of human rights? *Issues in Criminology* 5: 123–57.

———. (1977). Social class and the definition of crime. *Crime and Social Justice* 7: 4–13.

Scott, H. F., and Scott, W. F. (1982). *The Soviet art of war: Doctrine, strategy, and tactics*. Boulder, Colo.: Westview Press.

Sellin, T. (1938). *Culture, conflict and crime*. New York: Social Science Research Council.

Sherman, L. (1980). Three models of organizational corruption in agencies of social control. *Social Problems* 27: 478–91.

Shimoda et al. v. State of Japan (1963). District Court of Tokyo. Reprinted in Japanese Annual of International Law, 1964, 212.

Simon, D. R. (1995). *Elite deviance*. 5th ed. Boston: Allyn and Bacon.

Simon, H. (1964). On the concept of organizational goals. *Administrative Science Quarterly* 9 (June): 1–22.

Simpson, C. (1995). *The splendid blond beast*. Monroe, Me.: Common Courage Press.

Singh, N., and McWhinney, E. (1989). *Nuclear weapons and contemporary international law*. Boston: Martinus Nijhoff.

Skocpol, T. (1984). *Vision and method in historical sociology*. New York: Cambridge University Press.

Slusser, R. (1978). The Berlin crises of 1958–59 and 1961. In *Force without war: U.S. armed forces as a political instrument*, ed. B. Blechman, and S. Kaplan, 343–439. Washington, D.C.: Brookings Institution.

Steele, K. D. (1989). Hanford: America's nuclear graveyard. *Bulletin of Atomic Scientists* (October): 15–23.

Steffensmeier, D. (1989). On the causes of white-collar crime: An assessment of Hirschi and Gottfredson's claims. *Criminology* 27: 345–58.

Stewart, A. M. (1988). Low level radiation: The cancer controversy. *Bulletin of Atomic Scientists* (September): 15–19.

Stockwell, J. (1991). *The praetorian guard: The U.S. role in the new world order.* Boston: South End Press.

Stone, C. D. (1975). *Where the law ends: The social control of corporate behavior.* New York: Harper & Row.

Stone, J. (1954). *Legal controls of international conflict: A treatise on the dynamics of disputes and war law.* London: Stevens & Sons.

Stowell, E. C. (1945). The laws of war and the atomic bomb. *American Journal of International Law* 39: 784–88.

Sutherland, E. H. (1937). *The professional thief.* Chicago: University of Chicago Press.

———. (1940). White collar criminality. *American Sociological Review* 5: 1–12.

———. (1949). *White collar crime.* New York: Dryden.

Swing, J. T. (1991). *Right v. might: International law and the use of force.* New York: Council on Foreign Relations Press.

Tappan, P. (1947). Who is the criminal? *American Sociological Review* 12: 96–102.

Thomas, E. (1946). Atomic warfare and international law. *Proceedings of American Society of International Law* 40: 84–87.

Thompson, R. (1989). *Statement before the U.S. Congress, House.* Committee on Energy and Commerce. Subcommittee on Transportation and Hazardous Materials. Environmental crimes at DOE's nuclear weapons facilities. 101st Cong., 1st sess. Washington, D.C.: U.S. Government Printing Office.

Tifft, L., and Sullivan, D. (1980). *The struggle to be human: Crime, criminology, and anarchism.* Sanday, Orkney, U.K.: Cienfuegos Press.

Tilly, C. (1985). War making and state making as organized crime. In *Bringing the state back in,* ed. P. Evans, D. Rueschemeyer, and T. Skocpol, 169–91. Cambridge: Cambridge University Press.

Titus, A. C. (1986). *Bombs in the backyard: Atomic testing and American politics.* Reno: University of Nevada Press.

Truman, H. S. (1956). *Memoirs: Years of trial and hope.* Garden City, N.Y.: Doubleday.

Tucker, R. W. (1950). *The law of war and neutrality at sea*. Washington, D.C.: U.S. Government Printing Office.

Tunnell, K. D. (1993a). Political crime and pedagogy: A content analysis of criminology and criminal justice texts. *Journal of Criminal Justice Education* 4(1): 101–14.

——. (1993b). *Political crime in contemporary America: A critical approach*. New York: Garland.

Turk, A. (1982). *Political criminality: The defiance and defense of authority*. Beverly Hills: Sage.

Tushnet, M. (1988) *Central America and the law: The constitution, civil liberties, and the courts*. Boston: South End Press.

United Nations. (1980). *United Nations comprehensive studies on nuclear weapons*. Geneva: United Nations.

——. (1990). *Comprehensive study on nuclear weapons: Report of the Secretary-General*. Geneva: United Nations.

United States v. *Stanley*, 483 U.S. 699. (1987).

U.S. Atomic Energy Commission (1973). Report on patients injected with plutonium.

——. (1974). Fact sheet on plutonium injections.

U.S. Department of Energy (1979). DOE research and development and field facilities. Washington, D.C.: Oak Ridge Files.

——. (1984). Background information: Human experimentation projects involving human test subjects. Oak Ridge, Tenn.

——. (1995a). *Human radiation experiments: The Department of Energy roadmap to the story and records*. Washington, D.C.: U.S. Government Printing Office.

——. (1995b). *Human radiation studies: Remembering the early years: Oral history of Dr. Bain*. Washington, D.C.: U.S. Government Printing Office.

——. (1995c). *Human radiation studies: Remembering the early years: Oral history of Dr. Totter*. Washington, D.C.: U.S. Government Printing Office.

——. (1995d). *Closing the circle on the splitting of the atom*. Washington, D.C.: U.S. Government Printing Office.

U.S. Department of State (1984). *Foreign relations of the United States*. Vol. 15. Washington, D.C.: U.S. Government Printing Office.

U.S. Energy and Research Development Administration (1976). *Back-*

ground information on human testicular irradiation projects in Oregon and Washington prisons. Washington, D.C.: USERDA.

U.S. General Accounting Office. (1985). *Environment, safety and health: Environment and workers could be better protected at Ohio defense plants*. Washington, D.C.: GAO.

———. (1986). *Nuclear energy: Environmental issues at DOE's nuclear defense facilities*. Washington, D.C.: GAO.

———. (1989). *Dealing with enormous problems in the nuclear weapons complex*. Washington, D.C.: GAO.

U.S. House. (1986). *Litigation Relating to Atomic Testing*. Committee on the Judiciary. 99th Cong., 1st sess.

———. (1987). *Military medical malpractice and liability for injuries resulting from the atomic weapons testing program*. Subcommittee on Administrative Law and Governmental Relations. Committee on the Judiciary. 100th Cong., 1st sess.

———. (1990). *Health effects of radiation exposure*. Committee on Labor and Human Resources. 101st Cong., 2d sess.

———. (1993). *Environmental crimes at the Rocky Flats nuclear weapons facility*. Subcommittee on Investigations and Oversight. Committee on Science, Space, and Technology. 103d Cong., 1st sess.

———. (1994). *Radiation exposure from Pacific nuclear tests*. Subcommittee on Oversight and Investigations. Committee on Natural Resources. 103d Cong., 2d sess.

Vaughn, D. (1982). Toward an understanding of unlawful organizational behavior. *Michigan Law Review* 80: 1377–1402.

———. (1983). *Controlling unlawful organizational behavior: Social structure and corporate misconduct*. Chicago: University of Chicago Press.

———. (1996). *The Challenger launch decision: Risky technology, culture, and deviance at NASA*. Chicago: University of Chicago Press.

Vickman, L. (1988). *Why nuclear weapons are illegal*. Santa Barbara: Nuclear Age Peace Foundation.

Walker, D. (1986). *Statement before the U.S. Congress, House*. Committee on Government Operations. Subcommittee on Environment, Energy, and Natural Resources. Review of DOE's compliance with environmental laws in managing its hazardous and mixed radioactive-hazardous waste. 99th Cong., 2d sess. Washington, D.C.: U.S. Government Printing Office.

Weiner, T. (1990). *Blank check: The pentagon's black budget*. New York: Warner Books.

Westmoreland, W. (1980). *A soldier reports*. New York: Doubleday.

Weston, B. H. (1983). Nuclear weapons and international law: Prolegomenon to general illegality. *New York Law School Journal of International and Comparative Law* 4: 227–56.

———. (1983a). Nuclear weapons versus international law: A contextual reassessment. *McGill Law Journal* 28: 531–49.

What the president saw: A nation coming into its own. (1985). *Time*, July 29, 48–53.

Williams, R. C., and Cantelon, P. L. (1984). *The American atom: A documentary history from the discovery of fission to the present*. Philadelphia: University of Pennsylvania Press.

Wolfgang, M. (1972). *Delinquency in a birth cohort*. Chicago: University of Chicago Press.

World Health Organization. (1987). *Effects of nuclear war on health and health services*. Geneva: World Health Organization.

X [G. Kennan]. (1947). The sources of Soviet conduct. *Foreign Affairs* 25: 566–82.

Yin, R. (1984). *Case study research*. Beverly Hills: Sage.

York, H. F. (1976). The advisors: Oppenheimer, Teller, and the superbomb. San Francisco: W. H. Freeman.

Young, T. R. (1981). Corporate crime: A critique of the Clinard report. *Contemporary Crisis* 5: 323–36.

Zey-Ferrell, M., and Aiken, M. (1981). *Complex organizations: Critical perspectives*. Glenview, Ill.: Scott, Foresman.

Zinn, H. (1995). *A people's history of the United States: 1492–present*. Rev. ed. New York: HarperPerennial.

INDEX

Brookhaven National Laboratory, and human radiation experiments, 120
Bundy, McGeorge, 78, 79

Cabe, Ebb, 127
Cambodia, U.S. bombing campaign in, 91–92
capitalism: and nuclear threat, xii; and organizational crime, 146–47; and state crime, x
Carter, James Earl (Jimmy), 103
Castro, Fidel, 67–68
Ceauşescu, Nicolae, 85–86
Central Intelligence Agency, and human radiation experiments, 35
Challenger launch, 148
Chambliss, William J., 1; and definition of crime, 14–15; influence on study of state crime, 6
Chamoun, Camille, 66
Checkpoint Charlie confrontation, 67
Chiang Kai-shek, 41, 78
China: and communism, 46; communist revolution in, 41; and Eisenhower, 56, 61; and Korean War, 49–50; and NSC atomic weapons debate, 57; and nuclear weapons, 73, 77; and Truman, 53
Churchill, Winston, 58; and use of atomic weapons, 97
Clarfield, Gerard, 96
Clean Air Act (1970), 34–35, 109
Clean Water Act (1972), 34, 109
Clinard, Marshall B., 7
Clinton, William Jefferson (Bill), 118–19*n*
Coffee, John C., 7
Cohen, Albert K., 10
Cold War, 63; 1953–65, 65–69;

end of, 161–62; and Korean War, 39–42; and nuclear weapons production, 102, 112–13, 152; and state crime, xi. *See also* Soviet Union
Coleman, James S., 8–9
Coleman, James W., 147
Collins, J. Lawton, 52
Colson, Charles, 87
Columbia University, and human radiation experiments, 122
Comprehensive Test Ban Treaty, 165
containment: Eisenhower policy of, 65; Johnson policy of, 76
contamination. *See* environmental contamination
Conte, William, 139–40
corporate actors, 8–9
Cressey, Donald R., 9
crime: definition of, 12–13, 15; types of, 7. *See also* criminality; law; organizational crime; political white-collar crime; state crime
crimes against humanity (Nuremberg Charter), 32
crimes against peace (Nuremberg Charter), 32
criminality: classification of, 10–11; definition of, 5; environmental, 116–17; and organizational ethics, 158; and structural and organizational goals, 156; theories of, 143–44. *See also* crime; law
criminology: avoidance of nuclear issues by, 3–4; avoidance of state crime issues by, 5–6; identification of criminal behavior by, 11–13
Cuban Missile Crisis, 67–69, 102

customary international law. *See* international law

Cutler, Robert, 55

DEF CON system, 89

democracy, corruption of, x

Department of Corrections, Human Rights Review Committee, 139–40

Department of Defense: and human radiation experiments, 35, 36, 121; motivations of, 152–53

Department of Energy (DOE), 102–6, 120*n,* 123; contractor relationships with, 104–5; and environmental contamination, 113–14, 114–15; goals of, 157; human radiation experimentation database, 119*n;* and human radiation experiments, 35, 36, 121; and illegal activities of nuclear weapons production facilities, 111; monitoring of, 159; organizational management structure, 105–6; philosophy of nuclear weapons production, 115–17; and radioactivity regulations, 34–35, 109; Rocky Flats enforcement policy, 111

Department of Health and Human Services, and human radiation experiments, 35

Department of Veteran Affairs, and human radiation experiments, 35

deterrence, concept of, 75–76

deviance: criminal *vs.* noncriminal, 10–11; normalization of, 148

differential association theory, 143–44

DiIaconi, Daniel, 135

Dobrynin, Anatoly, 90–91

Dulles, John Foster, 58, 59–60, 62, 83

DuPont corporation, contract with Department of Energy, 104–5

Egilman, David, 130

Eisenhower, Dwight David: atomic strategy in Korea, 2, 42, 55–64; Atoms for Peace plan, 101; and Cuba, 67–68; and influence of public opinion, 159; and Nixon, 83; organizational goals of, 154, 157; and personal ethics, 158; personal goals of, 154–55; policy of containment, 65; and U.S. atomic stockpile, 49

Eisenhower Doctrine, 66

Elgin, Illinois, and human radiation experiments, 120

Ellsworth, Robert, 87

Energy Reorganization Act, 102

Energy Research and Development Administration (ERDA), 102–3, 120*n;* ethical guidelines for human subject research, 124–25

England, K. L., 133, 140

environmental contamination, 33–35, 106–12; motivations for, 153–54; and nuclear weapons production, ix–x, xi, 15, 16, 95–117; and organizational crime, xiii. *See also* radioactive and hazardous waste

Environmental Protection Agency (EPA): hazardous waste disposal regulations, 34–35, 109; raid on Rocky Flats facility, 110, 111–12

Ermann, M. David, 7, 8

Federal Bureau of Investigation (FBI), raid on Rocky Flats facility, 110
Felt, Harry D., 78–79
Fermi, Enrico, 95, 99–100
Fernald Feeds Materials Plant (Fernald, Ohio), 110
Fernald School, and human radiation experiments, 121
Finney, Henry C., 145–46
foreign policy. See Cold War; international law; specific countries
France, nuclear stockpile of, 73
Friedrichs, David, 1, 4, 6–7, 164

Geneva Conventions, 21, 22–23
Geneva Gas Protocol, 22–23
Genocide Convention, 21, 22–23
Germany: and Cold War, 66–67; and development of atomic weapons, 97, 98; parceling of, 39
Gerson, Joseph, 38, 152
Giddens, Anthony, 5
Glenn, John, 116
Gottfredson, Michael R., 144
governmental crime, definition of, 7
Great Britain: delivery of atomic bombs to, 50; nuclear stockpile of, 73; views on nuclear weapons, 51, 64
Greece, and Truman Doctrine, 44
Gross, Edward, 7
Groves, Leslie, 96, 98

Hague Conventions, 24, 26
Haldeman, H. R., 2, 83–84
Hall, Richard H., 8
Hamilton, Vernon L., 5
Hanford plant (Washington), x, 96, 105, 115; and human radiation experiments, 120; waste disposal practices, 107–8
hazardous waste. See environmental contamination; radioactive and hazardous waste
Heller, Carl, 133, 134, 135, 137
Henkin, Louis, 30
Hersch, Seymour, 87–88
Hiroshima: and legality of nuclear weapons, 19–20; Shimoda v. The State of Japan, 28–29; U.S. bombing of, 1–2, 3, 75, 97–98, 152
Hirschi, Travis, 144
Ho Chi Minh, 70
Hohn, Otto, 97
Holliday, Audrey, 139
Howland, Joseph, 127
human radiation experiments. See radiation experiments
human rights, concept of, 13–14
hydrogen bomb, development of, 48, 100–101, 113

Indochina, and communism, 46
informed consent, x, 123–24, 136, 140
International Court of Justice: Nicaragua v. The United States ruling, 31; and nuclear weapons, 2, 11, 14, 17, 39; and social control, 165. See also United Nations
international law: and crimes of the nuclear state, 15; customary, 24–29; and foreign policy, 156–57; and human radiation experiments, 140–42; and human rights, 14; and nuclear weapons, 16, 17–21; U.S. indifference to, 125; and violence of nation-states, 11. See also law; laws of war

Iran, Soviet support of, 40
Ivy, Andrew, 124

Jackall, Robert, 156
Japan: and atomic weapons, 97–98; federal court ruling, 25; and Korea, 43. *See also* Hiroshima; Nagasaki
Johnson, Louis, 48
Johnson, Lyndon Baines: and nuclear weapons, 76–82, 102; and Vietnam, 72
Joint Chiefs of Staff, recommendation on atomic weapons, 60–61

Kaku, Michio, 54
Kearns, Doris, 76–77, 80–81
Kelman, Herbert C., 5
Kennedy, John Fitzgerald: and Cuba, 67–69; and nuclear weapons production, 102; and Vietnam, 71–72
Khrushchev, Nikita, 44, 67
Kissinger, Henry, 84–88, 90
Klare, Michael, 162–63
Koons, Melvin, 133
Korea: and communism, 46; division of, 43
Korean War, 15, 16; and atomic weapons threat, 38–64; and Cold War, 39–42; Eisenhower's atomic strategy in, 2, 55–64; Nixon's views on, 83; political and military background of, 42–46; and state crime, 155; Truman's atomic strategy in, 49–55; and U.S. organizational goals, 154; U.S. threat to use nuclear weapons in, 29
Kramer, Ronald C., 4

Langham, Wright, 128
Lauterpacht, Hersh, 19

law: conventional, 22–23; legal framework for state crime, xii–xiii, 17–37; state violation of, 5; suits filed by testicular irradiation experiments victims, 138. *See also* crime; criminality; international law; laws of war
Lawrence Livermore Laboratory, and human radiation experiments, 120
laws of war, 18–21, 24, 26–27. *See also* international law
Lebanon Crisis (1958), 66
Lesieur, Henry R., 145–46
liberation movements, suppression of, x
Lifton, Robert Jay, *Hiroshima in America: Fifty Years of Denial,* 3
Lilienthal, David, 48, 100
Los Alamos National Laboratory, 96; and human radiation experiments, 120
Lundman, Richard J., 7, 8

MacArthur, Douglas, 49, 51, 55–56
Mai Van Bo, 86
Malott, Deane, 59
Manhattan Engineering District, 96
Manhattan Project, 40, 96–97, 120n; and compliance with Nuremberg Code, 129; and consequences of nuclear weapons production, 113–14; and human radiation experiments, 119–20; workers' exposure to plutonium, 125–26
Mao Tse-tung, 41
Marshall, George, 44–45
Marshall Islands, nuclear testing in, 122
Marshall Plan, 44–45
Marullo, Sam, 4, 153

Massachusetts General Hospital, and human radiation experiments, 122

Massachusetts Institute of Technology, and human radiation experiments, 121, 122

Matthews, Francis P., 52

McCarthyism, and nuclear weapons production, 102

McNamara, Robert S., 78, 79, 102

Merrick, George B., 111–12

Merton, Robert K., 145, 148

Meyrowitz, Elliott L., 25

Michalowski, Raymond J., ix–xiv, 146–47

Mitchell, Greg, *Hiroshima in America: Fifty Years of Denial,* 3

Mobilization for Survival, 108

Morris, Roger, 87

"mutual assured destruction" doctrine, 76

Nagasaki: and legality of nuclear weapons, 19–20; *Shimoda v. The State of Japan,* 28–29; U.S. bombing of, 97–98, 152

NASA, and human radiation experiments, 35

Nasser, Gamal Abdel, 66

National Academy of Sciences, 105

National Cancer Institute, 122

National Research Act, 125

national security, redefinition of, 162–63

National Security Council: and development of hydrogen bomb, 48; meeting (April 1964), 77–78; meetings (1953–54), 58–60; NSC-68, 45–46, 101; objectives in Southeast Asia, 71; report of November 1964, 79; on use of atomic weapons in Korea, 57–58

Nazis: Allied prosecution of, 31–33; genocidal practices of, 24; and nuclear weapons race, 97, 152; and Nuremberg Code, 35–36

Nehru, Jawaharal, 62

Nevada, nuclear testing in, 122

Newhouse, John, 46, 51–52

Ngo Dinh Diem, 66, 70

Nguyen Khanh, 77

Nguyen Van Thieu, 73

Nicaragua v. The United States, 31

Nitze, Paul, 46, 51–52

Nixon, Richard Milhous, 80n; and Eisenhower, 83; and influence of public opinion, 159; and November Ultimatum, 82–83, 88–89, 91–92; and nuclear weapons in Vietnam, 2, 82–92; organizational goals of, 154, 157; and personal ethics, 158; personal goals of, 154–55; on threat of atomic weapons use, 62

North Atlantic Treaty Organization (NATO): and first-use option, 75–76; and nuclear weapons, 73

Northwestern University, and human radiation experiments, 120

November Ultimatum, 82–83, 88–89, 91–92

nuclear outlaws, and nuclear threat, 162

Nuclear Regulatory Commission (NRC), 102–3

nuclear weapons: compared with atomic weapons, 38n; concept of deterrence, 75–76; expected effects of, 20; illegality of threat to use, 15, 29–33; illegality of use, 18–21; and international law, 16; and Johnson,

Russell, E. R., 127–28
Russia. *See* Soviet Union

Savannah River Plant (Aiken, South Carolina), x, 104, 106–7, 115; waste disposal practices, 107–8, 108–9
Schrager, Laura S., 7, 144
Schwartzenberger, Georg, 21
Schwendinger, Herman and Julia, 13
secrecy: and Manhattan Project, 96–97; and U.S. nuclear weapons program, 158–59, 165; in Vietnam negotiations, 84–85
Sellin, Thorsten, 12
Shaw, Simeon, 129
Shimoda v. The State of Japan, 25, 28–29
Short, James F., 7, 144
Sino-Soviet Defense Treaty, 41
Sitton, Ray, 89
Smith, Walter Bedell, 60
social control: and state crime, 164–66; and U.S. nuclear weapons program, 158–60
sociology: avoidance of nuclear issues by, 3–4; social-psychological theories of organizational crime, 143–44
Soviet Union: and development of atomic weapons, 98; and Eisenhower, 56; as imperialist threat, 54; and Korea, 43–44; and NSC atomic weapons debate, 57; and nuclear threat, ix, x; nuclear weapon capabilities of, 46–48, 74–75; as political and ideological competitor, 155; relations with U.S., 1960s–70s, 89–91; and Truman, 53. *See also* Cold War
Stalin, Joseph, 40, 41, 44, 54, 62

state: definition of, 4–5; as organizational actor, 9–10
state-corporate crime, definition of, 10
state crime, 4–15; and capitalism, x; causes of, 160–61; and Cold War, xi; controlling of, 161–66; definition of, 6–7; goals of, 153, 165; and individual complicity, 159–60; legal framework for, xii–xiii, 17–37; motivation for, 152–55, 161–62; and national security, 156, 162–64; opportunity structures for, 155–58; organizational theory of, xiii; and structural and institutional goals, 152–54; theories of, 143–48. *See also* crime; organizational crime; political white-collar crime
Steele, Karen D., 108
Stevens, Albert, 128–29
Stone, Christopher D., 7
Stone, Jeremy, 19
Stone, Jim, 110
Stone, Robert, 123
Stowell, Ellery C., 20
Strassman, Fritz, 97
Strategic Arms Limitation Talks (SALT), 69, 102
Suez Crisis (1956), 66
Sullivan, Dennis, 12
Sutherland, Edwin H., 7, 13, 143–44
Symington, Stuart, 52

terrorism, and nuclear threat, xii, 162
testicular irradiation studies, 119, 132–40; and informed consent, 136. *See also* radiation experiments
Thomas, E., 20
Tifft, Larry, 12
Tilly, Charles, 5

Tonkin Gulf Resolution, 72